Master William's Journal:

Tutoring Math and Science

Version 1.2

First Edition

I dedicate this journal to my family, as they have been there for me throughout my life. I am eternally grateful for my family's love and support; especially the little ones who have healed my heart and spirit countless times. I love you guys!

I also dedicate this journal to my friends, as they have kept my sanity in check during this chapter in my life. Here's to all the adventures we have had and to all the adventures that have yet to come.

I also would like to thank all the students I have tutored over the years and to all the students I have yet to tutor. It is because of my students that I was able to gain experience, passion, and knowledge to create this Math and Science Journal.

To all who read this journal: I hope this collection of Math and Science techniques proves useful throughout your Math and Science endeavors. And perhaps my recollection of being a Math and Science Tutor may inspire some to also become Math and Science Tutors.

Sincerely,

William Pappa

William Pappa

Master Math and Science Tutor

First Draft Start: March 20th, 2013

Second Draft Start: June 18th, 2014

Third Draft Start: April 14th, 2015

Final Draft Completion: Jan 17th, 2017

Table of Contents

Preface — 8

Brief Biography of Master William — 9

Recollection of Writing this Journal — 10

Introduction to Becoming a Master Tutor — 11

Master William's System of Tutor Levels — 12

Tutoring Virtues: Knowledge and Techniques — 20

Tutoring Virtues: Patience and Understanding — 24

    Endurance — 25

Tutoring Virtues: Insight and Kindness — 26

    Vigorous Practice versus Instant Insight — 27

Tutoring Virtues: Open-Mindedness — 29

Deeper Effects of Tutoring: Mental Fatigue — 31

Pre-Algebra Techniques — 33

Word Problems (Level One) — 38

    Reducing Fractions — 39

Linear Equations and Graphs — 43

Rules of Exponents — 47

Multiplying Polynomials — 48

Table of Contents

Factoring	49
Rational Expressions	56
Functions	60
Variance	61
Domain and Range	62
System of Linear Equations	63
Inequalities and Absolute Value	67
Intro to Pre-Calculus	69
Transformations of Functions	72
Word Problems (Level Two)	75
Quadratic Functions	77
Polynomial Functions	82
Asymptotes	83
Long Division	84
Polynomial and Rational Applications	85
Exponential and Logarithmic Functions	87
Intro to Trigonometry	89
Finding the Value of Trigonometric Angles	92

Table of Contents

Transformations of Trigonometric Functions   95

Trigonometric Proofs   98

Law of Sines, Law of Cosines, and Area of a Triangle using Trig.   100

Polar Coordinates and Vector Equations   101

Analytic Geometry   103

Sums and Series   106

Matrices   108

      Simplex Method   112

Linear Programming   120

Probability (Plus Venn Diagrams and Sets)   122

Basic Statistics   129

Finance   132

Limits   136

Differentiation   138

Integration   143

Conversion Factors   148

Significant Figures   151

6

Table of Contents

Nomenclature Basics of Chemistry   152

Stoichiometry   154

States of Matter and Basic Reactions   156

Aqueous Solutions   157

Thermochemistry   160

Basic Quantum Theory   162

Electron Configuration   163

Periodic Trends and Chemical Bonding   165

Molecular and Electron Geometry   167

Bond Order and Magnetic Properties   169

Gas Laws   170

Physical Properties of Liquids and Solids – Intermolecular Forces   173

Physical Properties of Solutions   176

Electrolytes   178

Kinetics   179

Equilibrium Basics   180

Acids and Bases   181

Acid-Base and Solution Equilibrium   185

Entropy and Free Energy   188

Table of Contents

Other Concepts within Chemistry   189

Basics of Physics   190

Word Problems (Level Three)   193

Let's Bake Some Cookies!   195

Learning Styles   201

Appendix A: Pascal's Triangle   204

Appendix B: Z-Table   205

Appendix C: Atomic Mass Unit List   207

Appendix D: Trigonometric Identities   209

Appendix E: Calculus Identities   210

Appendix F: Chemistry Equations   211

Appendix G: Physics Equations   212

Preface

The mind of a Master Math and Science Tutor can be quite perplexing. With many ideas and techniques, one must calmly sort the chaos through discipline. Furthermore, conveying such ideas and techniques to others can also be quite the challenge. Mastering both aspects are of great importance.

As the Master calmly meditates, he begins to hear the echo of droplets within the darkness. The Master begins to breathe to the rhythm of the droplets as he further deepens his trance.

Pondering further, the Master begins to recollect his experiences and categorizes his thoughts within a grid. The plane of memories are then analyzed and critiqued deeply to gather ideal techniques and strategies.

Such analysis must then be organized into a proper collection. Each individual story is then sketched onto pages that begin to surround the Master. With great care, the Master groups the collective canvases into a leather packet.

The Master then begins to open his newly crafted journal. As he begins his gaze into the journal-

"Hi. I heard you can help with me with Algebra. But I didn't want to bother you while you were reading."

The Master closes his journal. "Not a problem at all. I'd be happy to help you. So, what can I help with today?"

Brief Biography of Master William

My name is William Pappa, and I have been a Math and Science Tutor for over 10 years. Within that time, I have grown to become very passionate about being a tutor and I take great pride in teaching others, especially when the student leaves the tutoring session feeling more confident, becoming much stronger in command of the subject, and/or has broken mental barriers in an effort to improve themselves. As a matter of fact, I too have become far stronger in Math and Science through tutoring and teaching others.

I do have one confession. I did not start as a tutor with this in mind. In fact, the only reason for me becoming a tutor at first was to earn funding for my last semester's tuition. As I started tutoring, I noticed that my command was still strong in Math, but I had to formulate a method to relay my techniques to the students. I used my note taking skills and fused it with a mini lecture as an approach to teaching my students. This approach has been very effective in my experience as I can fine tune my techniques to each individual student's needs. The notes I wrote were then, and still are, given to my students as a point of reference. Before long, I had my funding for my tuition, but I remained as a tutor with the intension of keeping it as my main source of income. As I progressed as a tutor, I became passionate in teaching others.

As I tutored students throughout the years, I have gathered many techniques and skills that have been commonly effective for my students. Many techniques I remembered from my personal experience within the classes, but some techniques within this journal are from students themselves along with my own style and polish. I found that being open-minded to new techniques and to cater each student's needs, I was able to obtain many techniques. So many as I have written this journal as a collection of the most compatible techniques that my students have found most helpful.

Recollection of Writing this Journal

Writing this journal was enjoyable. I was quite surprised at the amount of techniques I was able to express. Granted, I could have constructed a textbook in much greater detail, but that would have been about 2000 pages or so long. But that's not the intension of this journal. Use this journal as a catalyst and not as a replacement for a textbook.

I wrote this journal not only to record many of the techniques I have learned over the years. This journal was more of a soul searching venture. I wrote this journal as an aid to any whom read it.

To all who read this journal, thank you. Spread the knowledge of this journal, and Math and Science in general, with the world and its children!

Author's Note: Once you start tutoring for as long as I have, you gain so much from the experience. Aside from the techniques and the sharpening of one's skills, I have gained the love and respect from so many students and colleagues. There are many students that appreciate everything that I do. Also, I appreciate my students who challenge me each and every day I tutor. Truly, without my students I would never have become such a strong tutor and a stronger person overall. And of course, without my students this journal would have never been created. To all my students, THANK YOU ALL!!!

Introduction to Becoming a Master Tutor

A Master Math and Science Tutor is not an easily obtained title. Before we dive into the inner workings of the Master, we should take a look at the basics of becoming a tutor.

First, a tutor should possess a good deal of knowledge and techniques in his or her preferred tutoring disciplines (such as Math, Chemistry, and Physics). With a strong knowledge background, the tutor can, in essence, be an effective tutor.

Second, a tutor should possess a good deal of patience and understanding in order to cater to everyone's individual needs. Everyone learns at difference rates and styles, so patience does help in regards to the tutor and his or her students.

Third, a tutor should possess a good deal of insight and kindness to invigorate his or her passion. Many aspects of the pursuit of knowledge (and in life in general) contain challenges that are not straight forward and require complex forms of thought and awareness.

Tutors whom take heart to these virtues and keep them well balanced within oneself will be able to obtain many students. Tutors that fail to embrace and improve these virtues may find themselves removing the title of tutor.

Being a tutor is not an easy task, especially with hordes of students pursuing said tutor. However, this becomes one of the signs that the tutor is beginning his or her journey in becoming a Master. Of course, the journey not only requires the tutor to strengthen these virtues, it requires the tutor to ascend upon them.

Master William's System of Tutor Levels

After nearly a decade of tutoring, the Master devises an interesting system in gauging tutors in levels of experience and aptitude. *(Author's Disclaimer: This system is from my own personal experience and my interpretation on the rate at which my skills as a tutor have improved.)*

Level	Hours of Tutoring Required
Grand Master	10,000
Master	5,000
Expert	1,000
Journeyman	500
Apprentice	250
Adapt	100
Beginner	0

Note: Master and Grand Master have addition requirements beyond the tutoring hour requirement.

When one aspires to become a better tutor, the Master believes this table will be a nice instrument to gauging oneself. Indeed, the tutor should study and keep this system as a pillar to one's self improvement.

This system is not meant to segregate tutors. Tutors should be devoted to helping others and each other in everyone's quest for knowledge.

In fact, any whom have a passion for teaching should be regarded as guardians in humanity's endeavor into enlightenment.

Master William's System of Tutor Levels

Beginner

Just as the name implies, beginner tutors have just started their tutoring journey. This tutor would not necessarily possess all three sets of tutor virtues, but would be eager to improve them as he or she begins tutoring.

A tutor at this stage starts with no informal training and little to no teaching methods. Tutors, in essence, have to practice tutoring as well as improving his or her virtues through tutoring. A rather counter-intuitive aspect compared to other professions, but tutoring is both an art and a science. The best way to becoming a better tutor is through experience.

As the tutor at this stage begins tutoring, he or she tends to gain his or her core teaching style. Tutoring styles can vary greatly between tutors and given situations, but the core theme should be established. The tutor also becomes acquainted with learning styles among students; noting Sensory Command (the Five Main Senses), Abstract Aptitude (Example: working with formulas), Imaginative Imagery (visualize the situation), and Theory Crafting/Execution (Example: formulate and implement the procedure in solving problems). (For more information regarding Learning Styles refer to pages 201-203.)

In improving one's tutoring virtues; the tutor begins to understand the various needs within students and begins to construct more specialized methods for certain situations. The list of specialized techniques has begun to materialize within our tutor.

Some tutors within this level may experience the need to improve select skills such as Scribe and Speechcraft. Improving one's Scribe skill allows one to articulate knowledge more effectively through illustrations. Improving one's Speechcraft also allows one to articulate knowledge more effectively through verbal cues. Once a tutor is able to fuse both skills into a single core style, he or she is on his or her way to becoming an effective and admired tutor.

Master William's System of Tutor Levels

Adapt

Adapt tutors would have a mild amount of experience and have established a slight possession towards at least one set of the tutor virtues. Tutors at this point are still in the learning chapter of tutoring.

A tutor at this phase would still not possess informal training, but the tutor would undoubtedly obtain a few teaching methods. The tutor begins to experience common questions asked from students. Common questions within the tutor's point of view would be lower level disciplines as the tutor has yet to tutor long enough to fully obtain all common questions within his or her discipline.

The core teaching style of the tutor has been roughly established, but should be sharped though practice. The tutor at this stage would have a fair understanding of learning styles within students and would have a few techniques within him or herself towards articulating knowledge.

Specialized techniques are still limited within the tutor at this level. More practice and experience would be required to obtain more specialized techniques as the tutor would still be mastering the tutor virtues.

Some tutors within this phase would begin to have a few devoted students to which commonly come to him or her for advice within the discipline rather than another tutor. Most students at this point are not quite confident asking for a tutor of this caliber, but that may change depending on the devotion and determination of the tutor.

Master William's System of Tutor Levels

Apprentice

Apprentice tutors are at the transition point between the learning chapter and established chapter in tutoring. Tutors at this phase would have a moderate amount of experience and a fair possession towards all three sets of tutor virtues.

At this point, the tutor may begin to obtain formal training and would have obtained quite a number of teaching methods. The common questions the tutor can answer have expanded to mid-level disciplines as the tutor has experienced a strong number of students. Although, the formal training can only be categorized as preparation for tutoring, and can never replace nor implement the virtues of tutoring. The virtues of tutoring must be obtained from tutoring experience.

The core teaching style of the tutor has been well established and only requires a moderate amount of improvement. The tutor should be able to analyze students and ascertain their respective learning styles fairly quickly. The number of techniques towards conveying knowledge has also increased.

Tutors within this phase have obtained a moderate amount of specialized techniques. Specialized techniques are more associated with the scale of the tutor's insight virtue. The kindness virtue would be used to drive oneself into mastering the specialized techniques for the students.

Some tutors at this level would have quite a few devoted students under his or her guidance. In fact, the majority of students would have confidence in tutors of this caliber.

Apprentice tutors may be able to tutor significant groups of students at the same time. Group tutoring must be practiced and viewed as a separate technique compared to the skill of tutoring one student at a time.

Master William's System of Tutor Levels

Journeyman

Tutors at this phase have a great amount of experience and a moderate possession of the three sets of tutor virtues. As such, journeyman tutors have become fairly established as tutors.

Common questions asked of the tutor have become natural to answer effectively and the range of common questions that can be asked has expanded throughout most of the tutor's desired discipline. Further expansion can be obtained with more tutoring experience.

The core teaching method of the tutor has been sharpened close to the point of mastery; which includes analyzing and determining learning styles within students. One particular core teaching method some tutors at this level have adopted would be a teaching method designed with mastering both the Scribe and Speechcraft skills. (This will be explained further on pages 21-23.)

Specialized techniques would be a focal point to tutors reaching this caliber. As students ask more questions, the questions become increasingly difficult. The issue that arises would be the students misinterpreting the tutor's ability to quickly answer common questions as being able to answer any question fast. This is when the tutor must begin categorizing the techniques and explanations into a notebook or journal as specialized techniques become far more numerous than the common questions.

Some tutors at this phase would have many devoted students under his or her guidance. At this point, the tutor becomes well known among the students. As a result, both aspects begin to push the tutor to his or her limit.

Group tutoring has been fairly established and used often when several students have the same questions. At this point, the group tutoring skill within the tutor is still rough and requires more practice.

Master William's System of Tutor Levels

Expert

Tutors reaching this plateau have a high amount of experience and a strong possession of the three sets of tutor virtues. Expert tutors have been well established as tutors in their respective disciplines.

The possible common questions that can be answered have already been experience by the expert tutor. New common questions can only arise with the new editions of texts within the tutor's desired discipline.

Expert tutors have a well-established core teaching method that has been sharpened to the point of mastery in the tutor's desired discipline. Improvements are possible for only small variations.

Specialized techniques would be the majority of the expert tutor's ability in conveying knowledge. The difficulty of the questions has increased and the number of questions has also increased. Expert tutors should have established a large notebook or journal containing many techniques as the sheer number of techniques can be overwhelming.

Only a few tutors would have a large number of devoted students under his or her guidance. Virtually all students would have confidence in tutors of this caliber.

The new issue for the expert tutor would be the ability to handle the hordes of students after his or her expertise. Such a task can push a tutor beyond their limits. In fact, group tutoring is not only mastered, but would be required.

Tutors that can push beyond their limits would have the chance to ascend their tutoring capabilities to even higher levels.

Master William's System of Tutor Levels

<u>Master</u>

Only with great determination, endurance, and mental discipline can a tutor ascend to a master tutor. At this ascension, the tutor has pushed beyond possessing the three sets of tutor virtues and has obtained a true understanding of the deeper meanings within the virtues. In fact, a new virtue becomes clear to the master tutor; the virtue of Open Mindedness. (This will be explained further on pages 29-30.)

Comparing to the other levels of tutors, the master tutor can answer virtually any question within his or her discipline(s) quickly and accurately. This is due to the immense experience required and the ability to push one's own limits well beyond the norm.

The number of students under a master tutor's guidance can be vast. Furthermore, some students may wish for guidance beyond the master tutor's primary disciplines.

One extra requirement for a master tutor would be the desire to help students in virtually any related discipline. Related disciplines such as Math and Physics, the master tutor who is well acquainted with one should take care in researching the other. The master tutor would teach him or herself the subject and return to the student with a strategy to convey the information and knowledge to the student.

Another extra requirement for a master tutor would be to write a book or journal containing the various techniques he or she has learned over the years. The book or journal would be a great reference point for both the master tutor and his or her students.

As for group tutoring, the master tutor would have the ability to essentially tutor an entire classroom of students. Not entirely a requirement for a master tutor, but this would be a needed skill nonetheless.

Master William's System of Tutor Levels

Grand Master

There are very few tutors who can reach this final level. A grand master tutor would have an immeasurable command over the tutor virtues and has a colossal amount of experience.

The amount of techniques within a grand master would be greatly difficult to contain as the grand master would have the ability to produce specialized techniques immediately as the students present their questions and material. With ever increasing difficulty of the questions asked, the special techniques become vast. No tome of knowledge can contain *all* knowledge!

Just like the master tutor, the grand master tutor's guidance can spread vastly. As such, some students ask the grand master questions beyond his or her related discipline.

One extra requirement for the grand master tutor would be the desire to help students in virtually any subject or discipline. At times, students may ask questions completely unrelated to the discipline(s) the grand master has become accustomed to. Unrelated disciplines such as Math and Psychology can be more difficult to transition between. Regardless of the unfamiliar discipline, as long as the grand master tutor has the *desire* to tutor, he or she can claim the title of grand master tutor.

Another extra requirement would be for the grand master tutor would be to make his or her book or journal accessible to his or her students and to many others. This can be done through publishing a physical book or journal, or through electronic formats.

Group tutoring can exceed the normal class size and the grand master tutor can perform in such a situation with great pride.

For those reaching this level, well done for all the hard work!

Tutoring Virtues: Knowledge and Techniques

Tutors must take care in perusing and preserving knowledge, and practice the techniques within various disciplines vigorously.

Knowledge can be obtained from various methods. One common form of obtaining knowledge would be from attending and observing lectures. Lectures are a classical form of instruction and can be quite effective depending on the teaching abilities of the lecturer. The tutor (or any student for that matter) may require another method of obtaining knowledge beyond lectures. Another common method would be self-teaching in the form of reading various texts within the discipline. Analyzing various text books can be overwhelming, but such a task is very common in one's pursuit of knowledge. Also, depending on the tutor, text, and discipline; self-teaching can be more effect than lecture.

Techniques can be obtained from vigorous practice and determination. This is especially true for disciplines with vast mathematical applications as such disciplines contain many techniques. In fact, this journal contains many techniques within Math, Chemistry, and Physics. The aforementioned disciplines possess many direct and indirect formulas within exercises that can require a great amount of insight to master. Many whom are reading this would find this information quite intense, but such a task is necessary to gather enlightenment within one's desirable discipline(s). Tutors have to articulate the techniques among such disciplines with great care.

Author's Note: There are many other disciplines that are not contained within this journal such as Astronomy, Biology, and English just to name a few. I am a master tutor within the subjects of Math, Chemistry, and Physics. As such, I have only contained my advanced techniques within those disciplines. Of course, I don't possess all the knowledge within these disciplines as, through my experience, virtually all students seeking tutoring are looking for guidance within the undergraduate levels of the aforementioned disciplines.

Tutoring Virtues: Knowledge and Techniques

Articulating knowledge and techniques can be difficult as all students learn at different rates and tend to have specific learning styles.

One vital skill tutors should master would be the Scribe skill. The Scribe skill in this regard would be the ability to write and draw illustrations clearly. Practicing such a craft takes time and patience. Here are a few examples with such clarity (Images are from the first draft of this journal):

(Ex1) Will makes a solution mixture from two concentrations of HCl: 10% and 50%. If Will wants the mixture to have a final concentration of 40% and a final volume of 20.0 L, how much of 10% and 50% are needed?

(Soln)

	Volume	× Concentration	= Total
Solution 1	x	0.10	$0.10x$
Solution 2	$20-x$	0.50	$0.50(20-x)$
Mixture	20	0.40	8

$$0.10x + 0.50(20-x) = 8$$
$$0.10x + 10 - 0.50x = 8 \qquad 5L \text{ of } 10\% \text{ HCl}$$
$$-0.40x + 10 = 8 \qquad 15L \text{ of } 50\% \text{ HCl}$$
$$-0.40x = -2$$
$$x = 5$$

(The above image is an example of a mixture problem.)

Tutoring Virtues: Knowledge and Techniques

(Ex) $\begin{cases} 5x + 6y \le 30 \\ 4x - 3y \ge 24 \end{cases}$

$5x + 6y = 30$ x | Y $4x - 3y = 24$ x | Y

$5(0) + 6y = 30$ 0 | 5 $4(0) - 3y = 24$ 0 | -8

$6y = 30 \to y = 5$ 6 | 0 $-3y = 24 \to y = -8$ 6 | 0

$5x + 6(0) = 30$ $4x - 3(0) = 24$

$5x = 30 \to x = 6$ $4x = 24 \to x = 6$

Test $(0,0)$

$5x + 6y \le 30$

$5(0) + 6(0) \le 30$

$0 \le 30$ True

$4x - 3y \ge 24$

$4(0) - 3(0) \ge 24$

$0 \ge 24$ False

(The above image is an example of graphing an inequality system.)

Not only is clarity vital in articulating the techniques, but the structure and organization are also of great importance. Primarily, the Scribe skill caters to students preferring visual explanations.

    The note taking aspect of the Scribe skill can be quite useful for students and tutors alike. Keeping a record of notes is of high importance since students and tutors can establish reference points within their respective disciplines.

Tutoring Virtues: Knowledge and Techniques

Another vital skill tutors should master would be the Speechcraft skill. The Speechcraft skill can be interpreted as the ability to clearly and calmly express the material in question verbally. Keeping a clear and calm voice can be quite challenging once the tutor's patience becomes stretched and worn down. The Speechcraft skill can be a derived skill more related to the next set of tutoring virtues, Patience and Understanding.

The style of the Speechcraft skill within each tutor may differ in one form or another. More specifically, the tone the tutor selects should be carefully considered. Softer tones tend to relax students more so than rougher tones, and confident tones tend to be preferred over stagnate tones in regards to student to tutor confidence.

Verbal content with the hand written notes can reinforce mental record keeping in regards to the study habits of students. Students can reread notes with the tutor's voice and tone in mind while studying, which can further justify the importance of both the Scribe skill and the Speechcraft skill.

Author's Note: The Speechcraft skill is helpful to relay techniques verbally and clearly. I have been told that my voice is very complementary to my style of tutoring since I use a clear, calm, and soothing voice. Combine both the Scribe and Speechcraft skills and you'll have an effective tutoring session. Most students seeking help through tutoring are usually a bit anxious and/or frustrated about specific material within the subject. Sometimes, students are just nervous about seeking help in general. This can be due to a common fear of asking help from someone superior in the subject. That's when both skills shine, with a clear explanation and a sincere nature; student(s) become more relaxed and confident about the material in question.

Tutoring Virtues: Patience and Understanding

Tutors are required to possess patience as the students seeking guidance would have yet to master the discipline in question. Patience can be considered as more of a characteristic trait to the tutor's persona, which can be obtained through tutoring experience. Often within tutoring sessions, the tutor may be expected to reiterate techniques several times to reinforce the information onto the student(s). Tutors should take care in considering the student's ability towards the discipline and his or her emotional state.

Improving one's patience would be an indirect approach in the form of knowing that the tutor has established the knowledge beforehand while the student has only begun to practice and study the discipline in question. Tutors should recall their own accounts of taking classes in regards to being sympathetic towards his or her students.

A large core within this set of tutoring virtues would be the tutor's emotional awareness. Students can be quite distraught from trying to balance the obligations categorized within social, employment, and college lives. The role of the tutor would be to not only articulate techniques onto the students, but to adjust tutoring strategies based off the student's current emotional state.

Increasing one's understanding directly relates to the tutor's experience. The tutor should obtain many different students through many sessions in order to observe students from various situations and environments.

Among all students and tutors, everyone learns at different rates; which should be referenced and expected as a tutor gains more students under his or her guidance.

Tutoring Virtues: Patience and Understanding

Endurance

Another core aspect would be the tutor's desire to strengthen his or her physical and mental endurance. Essentially, physical and mental endurance contributes to the tutor's ability to tutor for long periods of time. A tutor's overall endurance can be strengthened through their own experience and training.

The following is a table guide to a tutor's daily and weekly tutoring limits:

Level	Max Hours (Day)	Max Hours (Week)
Grand Master	14	60
Master	12	50
Expert	10	32
Journeyman	8	28
Apprentice	8	24
Adapt	6	18
Beginner	4	15

Endurance training can be difficult as the experiences specific to building this trait are not straight forward. Nevertheless, potential tutors should take note the table above as a reference point to improving one's endurance. Of course, some tutors may feel inclined to push beyond their currently established limit. Doing so, would increase the tutor's overall endurance even further.

Author's Note: I have pushed myself to crazy limits in regards to endurance. My personal tutoring record for a day is 15 hours and for a week is 60.5 hours. I mainly push myself to such lengths so I can tutor as many students as I physically can. However, I have noticed my overall endurance decreased as my mental health (See Page 31 on Mental Fatigue) began to decline. As the questions asked from students become more difficult (increasing in magnitude of the discipline, volume, and detail expressed), mental fatigue becomes a more common issue.

In other words: Endurance decreases as Mental Fatigue increases.

Tutoring Virtues: Insight and Kindness

The last set of tutoring virtues is more of a set of special traits within tutors. Insight is the tutor's ability to figure out exercises and applications involving critical thought. Tutors are able to obtain insight through vigorous experience practicing many different types of problems. Students may ask questions that require far more emphasis than direct explanation. Such questions can, and will, challenge a tutor's overall ability.

Clairvoyance of the various phases and the techniques associated that are possible within questions should be of great importance to the tutor. Unfortunately, tutors would obtain insight on their own through practice rather than through tutoring sessions. At times, the tutor may feel the need to meditate over the question(s) that he or she was unable to answer for the student due to the complexity of the question(s).

Author's Note: There have been many instances where I have been unable to answer a question asked by my student due to the lack of my awareness to the question. If the student was patient enough for me to meditate on the question for a brief period of time, I would eventually find the method to the question through a combination of research and my knowledge within the discipline. Otherwise, I practiced and researched the question on my own.

Once a tutor has gained enough insight, he or she becomes quite adapt to complex questions and the unique processes to solving such exercises. Combining the ability to solving simple and complex problems quickly can be very useful to the tutor; by extension, this would allow the tutor to help many students. However, once students feel that a tutor can answer such questions quickly, the students start to think that the tutor can answer any question quickly. Therefore, students tend to believe that the tutor would have the ability of instantaneous insight. This should not be the case as insight is obtained over time through the exercises within many disciplines.

Tutoring Virtues: Insight and Kindness

Vigorous Practice versus Instant Insight

Insight cannot be conveyed directly from tutor to student. Some students over time will obtain the perception of tutors being able to answer any kind of question regardless of discipline or difficulty. Especially when the students seek the help of a master tutor as he or she can be well versed within questions of multiple disciplines.

Author's Note: Through my experience as a master tutor, I have been expected to answer questions quickly. I have been able to achieve such a status not from satisfying the perception of the students, but from having to help many students in short periods of time and often in groups. There have been times where I was the only available tutor for Math and Chemistry having to help 30+ students during my shift. This was common place a few years ago as a "walk-in help" tutor. Answering questions quickly was more of a necessity during that time.

Commonly, tutors may be asked questions involving word problems. The main issue within word problems students have would be the ability to convert the words into calculations. Tutors are able to answer such questions due to having experience in solving many kinds of word problems. Expressing the unique techniques to word problems can be difficult depending on the complexity of the word problem and the current ability of the student.

Author's Note: In recent years, I have experienced a new kind of phrase from students. "What tells you to do that?" This question has become a pet peeve of mine. Granted, the phrase is not meant to be disrespectful, but such a question implies that tutors have an innate "cookie-cutter" strategy that we are keeping to ourselves. Trust me, I have tutored for over a decade and I can say that no such strategy exists. The question also implies that the student should not be required to use critical thinking. Unfortunately, most word problems are designed to have the student think about the scenario and to meditate on a method to solve the problem. Students are required to obtain their own insight through their own experiences.

Tutoring Virtues: Insight and Kindness

The other trait within this set of tutoring virtues is kindness. Such a trait is more specialized to a tutor's persona and past experiences.

Author's Note: As mentioned in my previous note about my pet peeve, I still attempt to explain the method and insight involved within the question. I understand the time limitation to learning a course within four months (or less) can limit a student's ability to obtain insight, but that can be argued as a time management issue rather than the discipline's difficulty. At this time, students seem to provide less and less time to learning and studying the material within the course, which allows less time to obtain insight. With that being said, I and other tutors still provide as much information and imagery as we can through illustrations and detailed steps within each word problem's unique process.

Students seek advice and guidance from tutors for various disciplines. Seeking such guidance can be intimidating at first as some students can feel anxious towards asking tutors questions. A common misconception some students have would be that the tutor would "look down" on those students due to the tutor's superior knowledge. This misconception can be easily eliminated through a tutor's kindness and emotional awareness. After a few tutoring sessions, a student becomes more comfortable with the tutor and far less anxious about the subject in question.

Author's Note: I have tutored many students from many walks of life. I have seen students driven to tears because they could not understand the material. This can especially be the case since if the student fails, they would lose something important to them in the form of losing a scholarship, dropping their grade point average, and/or losing the willpower to continue with college. When something is at risk, the student becomes far more stressed. I have tutored well past closing hours in order to help as many students as possible and to be curtain that my students had absorbed the material to give them the best possible chance to succeed.

Tutoring Virtues: Open-mindedness

The final tutoring virtue for tutors would be the ability of open-mindedness. This trait should be of great importance to tutors as having open-mindedness allows the tutor to observe and analyze student techniques and strategies. Tutors that expose themselves to more techniques and strategies will be able to adapt to virtually any student's specific learning style. As tutors experience many different learning styles, this allows the tutor to craft and enhance techniques that are commonly compatible among many students. Therefore, tutors should take care to obtain many techniques from tutoring sessions.

Another sub-trait within open-mindedness would be the tutor's ability to reconfigure techniques during a tutoring session. There are students that are very strict with using their own technique regardless of the possible flaws within the technique. As a tutor, modifying such a technique can be quite difficult as the tutor must provide exceptions or "patches" to the technique as to strengthen its usability.

Author's Note: Unfortunately, not all techniques students come up with are valid. Rarely I come across a student with a technique so flawed I was unable to provide any remedy for it. At that point, I relay a new technique that's as similar to the student's as possible. Usually, my student would accept my new technique after some demonstrations.

However, I have had a few students who were far too ensnared with their technique, simply refused to accept my new technique, claimed that their technique was superior, and/or resorted to insulting me. This is an extreme that I have experienced only a handful of times during my tutoring career, and in my experience those few are simply impossible to tutor. In a way, students should also have open-mindedness in order to master various techniques; which would allow tutors to become far more effective.

Tutoring Virtues: Open-mindedness

Tutors may experience students that insist to using the professor's (or teacher's) method to solving certain problems. Adapting to such techniques is vital to helping students as matching the professor's techniques would greatly reduce the chance of confusing the students. Sometimes the techniques students are given from the professor may not have been conveyed corrected. Such a scenario can often leave the tutor in a rather flustered position since the tutor may not know the specifics of the professor's technique. Tutors would have to attempt to construct a technique based on the limited information provided by the student and through the tutor's own experiences.

Author's Note: Most professors in my experience are open-minded to other techniques that the students may use for their classes. In fact, some professors utilize techniques that are compatible with most students and tutors. Still, I attempt to remain consistent to the professor's methods as much as possible.

An extra sub-trait to open-mindedness would be called translational tutoring. Translational tutoring essentially defines a tutor's ability to learn a concept within a discipline while tutoring a student. This ability is usually not obtained through experience and is usually a gifted talent within select tutors. As the tutor allows himself or herself to learn more subjects within a discipline (either through translational tutoring or traditional classes), he or she obtains more options for helping students.

Author's Note: During my tutoring career, I have had groups of students requesting help for classes beyond my expertise. One example was a specialized math course which required me to look up and practice concepts while tutoring students. A fair number of students involved in this practice have been very grateful for my desire to tutor a subject beyond my expertise. As a result, I have become familiar with several different disciplines due to my open-mindedness, kindness, and curiosity.

Deeper Effects of Tutoring: Mental Fatigue

Author's Note: After tutoring for over ten years, I have come to realize a very important issue; the issue of a tutor's mental state due to tutoring.

What I mean by mental state is more than just being mentally drained after a long day of tutoring; I also mean a tutor's emotional state. As tutoring is a very mentally demanding occupation, tutors should take heed in addressing this issue if and when it arises. Recently, I have noticed the effects of mental fatigue causing more harm to myself than I expected. As my tutoring ability becomes further tested, I began to notice my emotional state declining. Furthermore, as I mainly tutor in a walk-in center, I experience pressure in the form of being asked complex questions requiring a significant amount of time to convey, but without the option of time as there would be many other students waiting to be tutored in the same regard. With that said, I have come to realize a set of three primary variables within tutoring sessions that may explain my mental decline.

1. *Difficulty of the subject or discipline.*
2. *Student Cohesion*
3. *Tutor's Emotional State*

Tutoring in of itself can be difficult, but it seems that as the difficulty of the course being tutored increases, so does the amount of stress on the tutor. I can recall tutoring algebra with little effort as the exercises within did not require extraneous explanation. Compared to the subjects of Calculus, Chemistry, and Physics, the exercises required much more rigorous explanations. I suppose the correlation I am implying is that when the questions require deeper explanation, the tutor becomes more mentally strained. This can be especially true when the tutor is asked frequently for more detail of complex questions. One theme that has become more common would be that students request explicit detail about the tutor's thinking process and insight.

Deeper Effects of Tutoring: Mental Fatigue

As for student cohesion, this discusses the student's ability overall. This can expand onto, but not limited to, the student's analytical ability, memorization aptitude, time-management, physical and mental state. The student's ability to absorb knowledge from the tutor can vary drastically depending on the situation. I can express all the aforementioned abilities within students, but I cannot possibly include all possible outcomes; instead I will express a core issue. One interesting theme that has come up recently seems to be that students want tutors to convey insight fluently. I am unsure when students switched onto having the ideology of obtaining insight easily through the use of tutoring. I have listed before that insight cannot be taught or conveyed; one obtains insight through experience and practice.

I shouldn't have to explain why a tutor's emotional state is important. As students keep challenging my abilities with higher caliber questions, my mental state was drained to the point that tutoring began to damage my emotional state. It also does not help the fact that other things are happening in my life (as everyone has their own trials and tribulations) in which cause me to be less emotionally stable. I have taken measures to improve my emotional state such as being with family and friends, working on projects (such as this journal), playing video games, reading, and meditation. I suggest all who read this (anyone, not just tutors and students) to take care and keep one's emotional and physical states sound.

Interesting that I have listed insight commonly within the first section of this journal; but insight is very important in respect to life, not just studies. I also used disciplines to describe classes; this is in reference to studying martial arts as an implied metaphor. It takes time to develop martial arts. Studying Math, Chemistry, and Physics is not much different in that regard. One must practice these skills to master them. Only after much practice and determination can one obtain insight.

Pre-Algebra Techniques

Order of Operations

1. Parenthesis
2. Exponents
3. Multiplication and Division (left to right)
4. Addition and Subtraction (left to right)

The list above shows the priorities of Math Operators. The "left to right" note indicates the order of calculation as written out.

Parentheses are always done first. Actually, each set of parenthesis has its own Order of Operations to the effect of being its own equation. This effect can be chained within itself as when parentheses are within parenthesis; as such, follow and calculate the inner-most set of parenthesis and work your way out.

Exponents are calculated after parenthesis calculations.

The third is multiplication and division. This type of calculation should be done left to right, otherwise one risks miscalculation.

The fourth is addition and subtraction. Unlike multiplication and division, this calculation can be done in any order. The "left to right" method is still advised since the theme of calculation tends to prefer such methods.

Author's Note: The Order of Operations above follows the theme of problems which are written out on a single line horizontally. Addition and subtraction problems which are written out vertically, one number on top of the other, has an interesting rule. The magnitude (absolute value) of the number on the bottom must be smaller than the number on top.

Pre-Algebra Techniques

<u>Rule of Signs (Negative/Positive)</u>

Parenthesis: $+(+x) \rightarrow +x$ $\qquad$ $-(+x) \rightarrow -x$

$\qquad\qquad\quad$ $+(-x) \rightarrow -x$ $\qquad$ $-(-x) \rightarrow +x$

Exponents: $\qquad$ $(-x)^3 \rightarrow -x^3$ $\qquad$ $(-x)^4 \rightarrow +x^4$

$\qquad\qquad\quad$ $x^{-1} \rightarrow \frac{1}{x}$ $\qquad\qquad$ $\frac{1}{x^{-1}} \rightarrow x$

$\qquad\qquad\quad$ $\left(\frac{x}{y}\right)^{-1} \rightarrow \frac{y}{x}$ $\qquad$ $xy^{-1} \rightarrow \frac{x}{y}$ $\qquad\qquad$ $\frac{1}{xy^{-1}} \rightarrow \frac{y}{x}$

Multiplication and Division:

$(+)(+) \rightarrow +$ $\qquad$ $(+)(-) \rightarrow -$ $\qquad$ $(-)(+) \rightarrow -$ $\qquad$ $(-)(-) \rightarrow +$

Addition and Subtraction:

$(+) \ \& \ (+) \rightarrow +$ $\qquad$ $(-) \ \& \ (-) \rightarrow -$ $\qquad$ $(+) \ \& \ (-) \rightarrow +/-$

With Parenthesis, Multiplication, and Division: if the signs are the same, then the result will be positive; if the signs are different, then the result will be negative.

Involving exponents: if a negative value is taken as an even power, then the result will be positive; if taken as an odd power, then the result is negative. A negative exponent essentially causes the value/variable to switch between the numerator (top of a fraction) and the denominator (bottom of a fraction).

Addition and Subtraction calculation result is governed by the largest value between to two values. In other words, "keep the sign of the larger."

Pre-Algebra Techniques

Least Common Denominator (LCD)

1. Break down each value into prime factors.
2. Select the factors in common within each group, and then attach those factors onto the LCD once for each factor.
3. For the factors that remain, attach each onto the LCD.

$60 \rightarrow 2 \times 2 \times \mathbf{3} \times \mathbf{5}$ LCD: $\mathbf{3} \times \mathbf{5} \times 2 \times 2 \times 5 = 300$

$75 \rightarrow \mathbf{3} \times \mathbf{5} \times 5$

When figuring out the LCD involving variables and/or polynomials (two or more terms within parenthesis), the LCD will consist of each variable and/or polynomial and lists an exponent onto each equal to the number of times each variable/polynomial occurs at most within all denominators.

Example 1: $\dfrac{1}{x^2(x+4)} + \dfrac{1}{x(x+4)^2} + \dfrac{1}{2x}$ LCD: $2x^2(x+4)^2$

Common denominators (same bottom value) are required for addition and subtraction of fractions. However, when an equal sign is involved within an exercise with fractions, then one can multiply every term by the LCD to eliminate the denominators.

Example 2: $\dfrac{1}{2x} + \dfrac{3}{5x} + \dfrac{7}{10x} = \dfrac{9}{5}$ LCD: $2 \cdot 5 \cdot x = 10x$

$$10x\left(\frac{1}{2x}\right) + 10x\left(\frac{3}{5x}\right) + 10x\left(\frac{7}{10x}\right) = 10x\left(\frac{9}{5}\right)$$

$$5(1) + 2(3) + 1(7) = 2x(9)$$

$$5 + 6 + 7 = 18x$$

$$18 = 18x$$

$$x = 1$$

Pre-Algebra Techniques

Rules of Algebra (Master William's Simple Algebra Rules)

1. What you do to one side, you do exactly the same to the other side of the equal sign. (Keep in mind: a few special cases exist to this rule.)
2. To eliminate values away from "x", apply the opposite to both sides.
3. The objective of finding/solving for "x" is to get "x" by itself.
4. When figuring out the next step in solving for "x", think of using the Order of Operations but in reverse.

Ex. 3: Solve for x. $2(x-4)^2 + 5 = 23$

$$ -5 \quad -5 \qquad \text{Subtract 5 on both sides.}$$

$$2(x-4)^2 = 18$$

$$\frac{2(x-4)^2}{2} = \frac{18}{2} \qquad \text{Divide both sides by 2.}$$

$$(x-4)^2 = 9$$

$$\sqrt{(x-4)^2} = \pm\sqrt{9} \qquad \textit{Square root property}$$

$$x - 4 = \pm 3 \qquad \text{Separate into two equations.}$$

$$x - 4 = 3 \qquad\qquad x - 4 = -3$$

$$+4 \quad +4 \qquad\qquad +4 \quad +4 \qquad \text{Add 4 to both sides of each.}$$

$$x = 7 \qquad\qquad\quad x = 1 \qquad \text{Solution: } x = \{1,7\}$$

The square root property is used to eliminate the exponent surrounding the "x". Essentially, when one needs to eliminate a square exponent, then you take the square root of both sides. The special rule here is the addition of a plus and minus sign on the other side without an "x". This is required whenever one takes the square root of both sides as to compensate for the possibility of the quantity within the parenthesis that is squared being either positive or negative.

Pre-Algebra Techniques

Other Rules within Pre-Algebra

1. Distributive Property $\qquad$ $2(x + 4) \rightarrow 2x + 8$
2. Combine Like Terms $\qquad$ $2x + 3x = 5x$

Ex. 4: Solve for x. $\quad 4(x - 2) + 2x = 3x + 7$ $\qquad$ Distribute

$$4x - 8 + 2x = 3x + 7 \qquad \text{Combine Like Terms}$$

$$6x - 8 = 3x + 7$$

$$\underline{-3x \qquad -3x} \qquad \text{Subtract both sides by } 3x$$

$$3x - 8 = 7$$

$$\underline{+8 \ +8} \qquad \text{Add 8 to both sides}$$

$$3x = 15$$

$$\frac{3x}{3} = \frac{15}{3} \qquad \text{Divide both sides by 3}$$

$$\boldsymbol{x = 5} \qquad \text{Solution}$$

Author's Note: In the above exercise in line 4, I decided to subtract both sides by "3x" since it was the lowest value of the two "x" terms. This strategy is effective in reducing the number of negative values involved. As a nice reference, the lowest "x" term being the lowest positive or the strongest negative. In the case of a negative "x" term, add that value to both sides to eliminate it.

Students and tutors alike must practice the Math concepts to master them. There is NO EXCEPTION to this rule. Math is a skill one must practice vigorously to master. Granted, there are people in the world whom are very keen to Math, but they require practice as well. Just thought I would mention this piece of wisdom before proceeding further.

Word Problems (Level One)

<u>Types of Level One Word Problems</u>

1. Basic equation or "plug-and-chug"
2. Distance $\qquad\qquad d = rt$
3. Simple Interest $\qquad\quad I = Prt$
4. Mixture

Basic equation or "plug-and-chug"

Ex 1: One number is 6 more than another number; their sum is 24. What are the two numbers?

Work: Smaller number = x Larger number = $x + 6$

$(x) + (x + 6) = 24$ For $x = 9 \rightarrow (9) + 6 \rightarrow 15$

$2x + 6 = 24$

$2x = 18$

$x = 9$

Solution: **The two numbers are 9 and 15.**

Ex 2: Find the Area and Perimeter of a rectangle with length of 8 feet and width of 6 feet. (Area is Length times Width, and Perimeter is the sum of all sides.)

Work: Length = 8 feet Width = 6 feet

$A = L \cdot w$ $\qquad\qquad P = 2L + 2w$ $\qquad\qquad$ 6

$A = (8 \text{ ft})(6 \text{ ft})$ $\qquad P = 2(8 \text{ ft}) + 2(6 \text{ ft})$ $\qquad$ 8

$A = \mathbf{48 \text{ ft}^2}$ $\qquad\qquad P = 16 \text{ ft} + 12 \text{ ft}$

$\qquad\qquad\qquad\qquad\qquad P = \mathbf{28 \text{ ft}}$

Word Problems (Level One)

Distance = Rate x Time $\qquad$ $d = rt$

Ex 3: Two cars leave a city at the same time. One drives east at 50 miles per hour and the other drives west at 60 miles per hour. How long will it take for the two cars to be 275 miles apart?

Work:

	Rate	Time	Distance
Eastbound	50	x	$50x$
Westbound	60	x	$60x$
Total			275

$50x + 60x = 275$ $\qquad$ Add both distances to equal the total

$110x = 275$ $\qquad$ Combine Like Terms

$x = \frac{275}{110} \to \frac{55}{22} \to \frac{5}{2}$ Or $2\frac{1}{2}$ $\qquad$ Reduce the resulting fraction

Solution: **The two cars will be 275 miles apart in $\frac{5}{2}$ hours, or in $2\frac{1}{2}$ hours.**

In the above example, the solution had a large value fraction which was reduced to a more manageable fraction. In order to reduce fractions, one would divide the top and bottom of the fraction by a common factor (a value that divides evenly with each number).

Divisible by...	Rule set for each factor (Ref: the number in question)
2	Ends in an even number.
3	Sum of the digits of the number equals a multiple of 3.
5	Ends in ether '0' or '5.'
7	2(hundreds) + 3(tens) + (ones) = multiple of 7. (except 4+ digit #'s)

Beyond the above factors, one can use larger prime numbers to see if the numbers can be reduced further. Other rule sets exist for multiples of 4, 6, 8, 9, and 10, but the above list can be used in spite of them.

Word Problems (Level One)

Simple Interest = Principle x Rate x Time $\qquad I = Prt$

Ex 4: Myrandah invests some money at 6% simple interest and invests $100 more than that amount at 8% simple interest. Over 3 years, the interest earned was $129. How much did Myrandah invest in each rate?

Work:

	Principle	Rate	Time	Interest
Investment 1	x	0.06	3	$0.18\,x$
Investment 2	$x + 100$	0.08	3	$0.24\,(x + 100)$
				129

$0.18x + 0.24(x + 100) = 129$ $\qquad$ Add both interests to equal the total

$0.18x + 0.24x + 24 = 129$ $\qquad$ Distribute and Combine Like Terms

$0.42x + 24 = 129$ $\qquad$ Subtract both sides by 24

$0.42x = 105$ $\qquad$ Divide both sides by 0.42

$x = 250$ $\qquad$ In calculator: $105 \div 0.42 = 250$

$x + 100 \rightarrow (250) + 100 \rightarrow 350$ $\qquad$ Plug in x to find the other Principle

Solution: **Myrandah invested $250 in the 6% rate and $350 in the 8% rate.**

Similar to the previous page, within the last column one would add the first two row results and set them equal to the last row result. This is also done with Mixture problems on the next page. Adding these values is due to the situation within each having logically additive characteristics. For instance, with Example 3 on page 39, the two distances were added together since the cars are going in opposite directions. If the cars were heading in the same direction, one would have taken the difference between the two distances.

Word Problems (Level One)

Mixture   Volume x Concentration = Total

Ex 5: Will wants to form a solution mixture from two concentrations of hydrochloric acid; 10% and 50%. If Will wants the mixture to have a final concentration of 40% and a final volume of 20.0 liters, how many liters of 10% and 50% must be mixed to obtain the desired concentration?

Work:

	Volume	Concentration	Total
Solution 1	x	0.10	$0.10x$
Solution 2	$20 - x$	0.50	$0.50(20 - x)$
Mixture	20	0.40	8

$0.10x + 0.50(20 - x) = 8$ Add both Solutions equal to Mixture

$0.10x + 10 - 0.50x = 8$ Distribute and Combine Like Terms

$-0.40x + 10 = 8$ Subtract both sides by 10

$-0.40x = -2$ Divide both sides by -0.40

$x = 5$ In calculator: $-2 \div (-0.40) = 5$

$20 - x \rightarrow 20 - (5) \rightarrow 15$ Plug in x to obtain the second volume

Solution: **Will mixes 5 liters of 10% hydrochloric acid with 15 liters of 50% hydrochloric acid to obtain his desired mixture.**

The volume of the 50% solution was obtained as "$20 - x$." This is due to the total volume of the resulting mixture of both solutions being 20 liters and declaring an "x" amount of liters for the amount of the 10% solution. The difference between the mixture volume and the 10% solution volume would yield the volume of the 50% solution.

Word Problems (Level One)

Word problems are quite interesting. They show one the application aspects of Math. However, the main issue students have with word problems would be the ability to translate words into Math. Unfortunately, there is no "cookie-cutter" strategy for all word problems, but there are some strategies and procedures that can be used and implemented depending on the situation.

Word Problem Strategies

1. Figure out what type of word problem you are dealing with (Distance, Mixture, etc.). If the word problem follows a certain type, follow out the steps of that type.
2. Visualize the situation the word problem is declaring. Even drawing an illustration of the situation can help with the logic of the word problem.
3. Construct a Data Table to categorize and match the variables in the word problems. (Evident in Examples 3, 4, and 5 within this chapter.)

Due to the nature of word problems, one must logically devise a plan of action to solve the problem rather than trying to find a "cookie-cutter" approach to all word problems. There are just far too many types of word problems to construct such a strategy.

Author's Note: I can recall many times when my students would ask me about a "cookie-cutter" strategy for word problems. The subject of word problems is a vast one. In fact, I have labeled word problems in three levels within this journal. Level two word problems contain more complexity with adding more variables to solve for and are usually not as direct as level one word problems. Level three word problems mostly consists of Science questions as they require insight and are often multi-typed word problems. Nevertheless, the above strategies can be useful in aiding you with virtually any word problem.

Linear Equations and Graphs

Types of Linear Equations

1. Slope $\qquad m = \frac{y_2 - y_1}{x_2 - x_1} \qquad m = \frac{rise}{run}$

2. Slope-Intercept $\qquad y = mx + b$

3. Point-Slope $\qquad y - y_1 = m(x - x_1)$

4. Standard Form $\qquad Ax + By = C$

(As A, B, and C are integers, and A is positive.)

Slope is the rate of change of the ratio of y to x. In other words, the top value ($rise$) declares how far upward (positive slope) or how far downward (negative slope) and the bottom value (run) declares how far to the right each point is to each other. One can graph a line knowing slope and a starting point.

Slope-Intercept can be written out when slope (m) and y-intercept (b) are known [Ex: $m = 2, b = 3 \rightarrow y = 2x + 3$]. Also, this form is quite ideal in graphing lines since the y-intercept acts as the starting point and new points can be obtained using slope.

Point-Slope can be written out when slope (m) and a point (x_1, y_1) are known [Ex: $m = 2, p(3,4) \rightarrow y - 4 = 2(x - 3)$]. Solving for '$y$' in Point-Slope form will result in the Slope-Intercept form, "$y = mx + b$."

Standard Form is only used if the directions within the problem state to answer in "standard form." There is another variation to this equation called General Form which is usually designated as setting the equation equal to zero ($Ax + By + C = 0$).

Linear Equations and Graphs

Graphing Methods

1. Slope and Starting Point
2. Use x and y intercepts (where the line crosses the x and y axis)
3. Vertical and Horizontal Lines

Slope and Starting Point

Ex 1: Graph the equation, $y = \frac{3}{2}x - 4$.

Work: The slope has a rise of 3 and a run of 2, and the y-intercept (our starting point) has a value of -4. First, plot a point at the -4 value of the y-axis. Next, rise up by 3 then run to the right by 2 and plot another point. Finally, connect the dots and extend the line to the edges to complete the line.

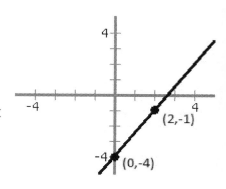

Use x and y Intercepts

Ex 2: Graph the equation, $2x + 3y = 12$

Work: To find the x-intercept, set $y = 0$.

$2x + 3(0) = 12$

$2x = 12$

$x = 6$ → x-intercept: (6,0)

To find the y-intercept, set $x = 0$

$2(0) + 3y = 12$

$3y = 12$

$y = 4$ → y-intercept: (0,4)

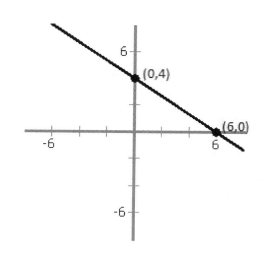

Linear Equations and Graphs

Vertical and Horizontal Lines (Special types of linear equations):

Vertical Lines

Equation: $x = c$ Slope: *undefined*

Horizontal Lines

Equation: $y = c$ Slope: $m = 0$

Some exercises may not give one the slope directly. When this happens, follow the rules from this chapter along with the following two rules:

1. Parallel Lines (‖) have the same slope.
2. Perpendicular Lines (⊥) have negative reciprocal slopes. In other words, take the known slope: switch the sign and flip the fraction.

Ex 3: Find the equation of a line that passes through the point $(2,5)$ and is parallel to the equation $2x + 3y = 6$.

Work: Find the slope of the given equation. Next, plug in both the point and the slope into the Point-Slope equation and simply to Slope-Intercept form.

$$2x + 3y = 6 \qquad\qquad y - (5) = \left(-\frac{2}{3}\right)(x - 2) \qquad y - y_1 = m(x - x_1)$$

$$3y = -2x + 6 \qquad\qquad y - 5 = -\frac{2}{3}x + \frac{4}{3}$$

$$y = -\frac{2}{3}x + 2 \qquad\qquad y = -\frac{2}{3}x + \frac{4}{3} + 5$$

$$m = -\frac{2}{3} \qquad\qquad y = -\frac{2}{3}x + \frac{4}{3} + \frac{15}{3}$$

$$\left\{ y = -\frac{2}{3}x + \frac{19}{3} \right\} \qquad\qquad y = mx + b$$

Linear Equations and Graphs

Ex 4: Find the equation of a line that passes through the point $(3, -4)$ and is perpendicular to the equation $y = -\frac{2}{3}x + \frac{10}{9}$.

Work: Find the slope of the given equation, switch the sign and flip the fraction to obtain the desired slope. Next, plug in both the point and the slope into the Point-Slope equation and simply to Slope-Intercept form.

$$y = -\frac{2}{3}x + \frac{10}{9} \qquad\qquad y - (-4) = \left(\frac{3}{2}\right)(x - 3) \qquad\qquad y - y_1 = m(x - x_1)$$

$$m = -\frac{2}{3} \qquad\qquad\qquad y + 4 = \frac{3}{2}x - \frac{9}{2}$$

$$m_\perp = +\frac{3}{2} \qquad\qquad\qquad y = \frac{3}{2}x - \frac{9}{2} - 4$$

$$y = \frac{3}{2}x - \frac{9}{2} - \frac{8}{2}$$

$$\left\{ y = \frac{3}{2}x - \frac{17}{2} \right\} \qquad\qquad\qquad y = mx + b$$

Rules of Exponents

1. $x^m \cdot x^n = x^{m+n}$ Multiplying like bases with exponents

2. $\frac{x^m}{x^n} = x^{m-n}$ Dividing like bases with exponents

3. $(x^m)^n = x^{mn}$ Exponent Chain

4. $x^{-m} = \frac{1}{x^m}$ Negative Exponent

5. $x^0 = 1$ Power of Zero

Multiply like bases with exponents: Add the exponents.

Ex 1: $x^3 \cdot x^4 \rightarrow x^{3+4} \rightarrow \{x^7\}$

Dividing like bases with exponents: Subtract the exponents.

Ex 2: $\frac{x^6}{x^4} \rightarrow x^{6-4} \rightarrow \{x^2\}$

Exponent Chain: Exponents outside of parenthesis of an expression without addition or subtraction and contain an exponential term. Multiply, or in some cases distribute, the outside exponent with the exponent(s) inside.

Ex 3: $(x^3y^2)^4 \rightarrow x^{3 \cdot 4}y^{2 \cdot 4} \rightarrow \{x^{12}y^8\}$

Negative Exponents: Switch the base and exponent between numerator and denominator to remove the negative sign from the exponent.

Ex 4: $\left(\frac{x^{-2}y^3}{z^{-4}}\right)^5 \rightarrow \left(\frac{z^4y^3}{x^2}\right)^5 \rightarrow \frac{z^{4 \cdot 5}y^{3 \cdot 5}}{x^{2 \cdot 5}} \rightarrow \left\{\frac{z^{20}y^{15}}{x^{10}}\right\}$

Power of Zero: Anything to the power of zero equals one.

Multiplying Polynomials

1. FOIL Method   (two term by two term)
2. Box Method   (more than two terms in one or both expressions)

The FOIL Method can be translated as "First, Outer, Inner, and Last." This method is useful as an intro to multiplying polynomials.

Ex 1: $(2x + 3)(4x + 5)$

First   Outer   Inner   Last

$(2x)(4x) +$ $(2x)(5) +$ $(3)(4x) +$ $(3)(5)$

$8x^2 + 10x + 12x + 15$

$\{8x^2 + 22x + 15\}$

The Box Method is more applicable when more than two terms are within either or both parenthesis.

Ex 2: $(2x + 3)(4x^2 + 5x + 6)$

	$4x^2$	$5x$	6
$2x$	$8x^3$	$10x^2$	$12x$
3	$12x^2$	$15x$	18

$8x^3 + 10x^2 + 12x + 12x^2 + 15x + 18$

$\{8x^3 + 22x^2 + 27x + 18\}$

The Box Method may look more appealing than the FOIL Method, but students should master both the FOIL Method and Box Method in order to judge which between the two would be the quicker method within specific exercises.

Factoring

Types of Factoring

1. Minor Factoring (Greatest Common Factor or GCF)
2. Factoring by Grouping
3. Major Factoring (without leading coefficient)
4. Major Factoring (with leading coefficient)
5. Special Factoring

Author's Note: Before we dive into factoring, I want to make this clear. Fully absorb this chapter. Factoring is a Math skill that will be needed in virtually all levels of Math. This includes Trigonometry and Calculus!

Minor Factoring (GCF) – Factoring out the GCF from all terms is the first step of factoring. The GCF will contain the greatest common multiple between the coefficients and the lowest exponent of any common variables or expressions that are shared within all original terms.

Ex 1: Factor: $2x^2 + 4x$

   GCF: $2x$

   $\{2x(x + 2)\}$

Ex 2: Factor: $12x^4 - 16x^3 + 24x^2$

   GCF: $4x^2$

   $\{4x^2(3x^2 - 4x + 6)\}$

Ex 3: Factor: $27x^3 + 3x + 9y$

   GCF: 3

   $\{3(9x^3 + x + 3y)\}$

Ex 4: Factor: $5x^7y^4 + 10x^5y^3$

   GCF: $5x^5y^3$

   $\{5x^5y^3(x^2y + 2)\}$

Factoring

Factoring by Grouping – Given a set of four terms, proceed with Minor Factoring for the first two terms and the last two terms as two separate groups. Check the resulting terms inside the parenthesis. If the terms in each set of parenthesis are the same, then group the outer terms inside a set of parenthesis next to one set of the checked expression from the previous step.

Ex 5: Factor: $3x^2 + 6x + 4x + 8$

$3x(x + 2) + 4(x + 2)$

$\{(3x + 4)(x + 2)\}$

Ex 6: Factor: $5x^2 - 15x - 7x + 21$

$5x(x - 3) - 7(x - 3)$

$\{(5x - 7)(x - 3)\}$

Ex 7: Factor: $5x^2 + 20xy - 8xy - 32y^2$

$5x(x + 4y) - 8y(x + 4y)$

$\{(5x - 8y)(x + 4y)\}$

Note: Notice in exercises 6 and 7 that the third term is negative. When this occurs, it is ideal to factor out the negative from the last two terms. This will leave the first term inside the parenthesis as positive, which is usually required in matching with the other set of parenthesis.

Factoring

Majoring Factoring (without leading coefficient) – When factoring a trinomial (three term expression) without a leading coefficient, set up two sets of parenthesis each with the leading term of the trinomial as the first term, but as a square root version of itself. Find two values which when multiplied gives the last coefficient of the trinomial AND when combined (add/subtract) gives the middle coefficient of the trinomial. If the last term has a variable within itself, apply the similar effect to that term as was done with the first term of the trinomial.

Ex 8: Factor: $x^2 + 6x + 8$

(x + _)(x + _)

$8 \rightarrow (4)(2)$

$4 + 2 \rightarrow 6$

$\{(x + 4)(x + 2)\}$

Ex 9: Factor: $x^2 - 5x + 6$

(x − _)(x − _)

$6 \rightarrow (-2)(-3)$

$-2 - 3 \rightarrow -5$

$\{(x - 2)(x - 3)\}$

Ex 10: Factor: $x^2 + 7xy - 18y^2$

(x + _ y)(x − _ y)

$-18 \rightarrow (9)(-2)$

$9 - 2 \rightarrow 7$

$\{(x + 9y)(x - 2y)\}$

Ex 11: Factor: $x^2 - 8xy - 33y^2$

(x − _ y)(x + _ y)

$-33 \rightarrow (-11)(3)$

$-11 + 3 \rightarrow -8$

$\{(x - 11y)(x + 3y)\}$

Factoring

Major Factoring (with leading coefficient) – When factoring a trinomial with a leading coefficient, the first step is to multiply the leading coefficient with the last term. Find two values when multiplied gives the resulting product from before AND when combined gives the middle term of the trinomial. Then replace the middle term with the two values found in the previous step, and proceed with Factoring by Grouping to finish factoring the trinomial.

Ex 12: Factoring: $6x^2 + 13x + 6$

$(6)(6) \rightarrow 36$

$36 \rightarrow (9)(4)$

$9 + 4 \rightarrow 13$

$6x^2 + 9x + 4x + 6$

$3x(2x + 3) + 2(2x + 3)$

$\{(3x + 2)(2x + 3)\}$

Ex 13: Factor: $8x^2 + 14x - 15$

$(8)(-15) \rightarrow -120$

$-120 \rightarrow (20)(-6)$

$20 - 6 \rightarrow 14$

$8x^2 + 20x - 6x - 15$

$4x(2x + 5) - 3(2x + 5)$

$\{(4x - 3)(2x + 5)\}$

Ex 14: Factor: $35x^2 - 62xy + 24y^2$

$(35)(24) \rightarrow 840$

$840 \rightarrow (-42)(-20)$

$-42 - 20 \rightarrow -62$

$35x^2 - 42xy - 20xy + 24y^2$

$7x(5x - 6y) - 4y(5x - 6y)$

$\{(7x - 4y)(5x - 6y)\}$

Factoring

Special Factoring – Three special factoring situations.

1. Difference of two squares: $x^2 - y^2 = (x + y)(x - y)$
2. Sum of two cubes: $x^3 + y^3 = (x + y)(x^2 - xy + y^2)$
3. Difference of two cubes: $x^3 - y^3 = (x - y)(x^2 + xy + y^2)$

Ex 15: Factor: $4x^2 - 9y^2$

$(2x)^2 - (3y)^2$ $\qquad\qquad\qquad\qquad$ $x^2 - y^2$

$\{(2x + 3y)(2x - 3y)\}$ $\qquad\qquad\qquad$ $(x + y)(x - y)$

Ex 16: Factor: $8x^3 + 27y^3$

$(2x)^3 + (3y)^3$ $\qquad\qquad\qquad\qquad$ $x^3 + y^3$

$(2x + 3y)((2x)^2 - (2x)(3y) + (3y)^2)$ $\qquad$ $(x + y)(x^2 - xy + y^2)$

$\{(2x + 3y)(4x^2 - 6xy + 9y^2)\}$

Ex 17: Factor: $64x^3 - 125y^3$

$(4x)^3 - (5y)^3$ $\qquad\qquad\qquad\qquad$ $x^3 - y^3$

$(4x - 5y)((4x)^2 + (4x)(5y) + (5y)^2)$ $\qquad$ $(x - y)(x^2 + xy + y^2)$

$\{(4x - 5y)(16x^2 + 20xy + 25y^2)\}$

Factoring

Notice with Special Factoring, the first step is to square root or cube root the terms into a different notation. This notation comes in handy for placing the terms within the Special Factoring equations. The following table contains the squares and cubes of the first 20 numbers.

x	x^2	x^3	x	x^2	x^3
1	1	1	11	121	1331
2	4	8	12	144	1728
3	9	27	13	169	2197
4	16	64	14	196	2744
5	25	125	15	225	3375
6	36	216	16	256	4096
7	49	343	17	289	4913
8	64	512	18	324	5832
9	81	729	19	361	6859
10	100	1000	20	400	8000

Author's Note: I suggest memorizing all 20 squares and the first 10 cubes to help with Special Factoring, square roots, and cube roots.

Factoring

When figuring out the two values to use for Major Factoring, consider the following tips:

1. When the last term or resulting product is positive, the combination will be the sum of the two values and these values will have the same sign.
2. When the last term or resulting product is negative, the combination will be the difference of the two values and these values will have different signs.

Author's Note: About seven years ago, I came across a student with heavy trouble with factoring with a short period of time to master factoring. I then showed him the method of Major Factoring with coefficients, and he was able to apply it to all forms of factoring with the exception of the sum and difference of two cubes. Not really recommended for all due to time constrains and the moderate insight required foreseeing the values to use.

Above all, students and tutors alike need to practice factoring vigorously to keep it sharp. Factoring will be needed in future sections and classes. I cannot stress this enough.

Rational Expressions

The following example shows the procedure on simplifying Rational Expressions. Not all Rational Expressions contain the same number of steps in this example, but this method should still be referenced when simplifying Rational Expressions.

Ex 1: Simplify: $\dfrac{6x^2-x-12}{2x^2+11x+12} \div \dfrac{6x^2-17x+12}{2x^2+7x+6}$

$\dfrac{6x^2-x-12}{2x^2+11x+12} \cdot \dfrac{2x^2+7x+6}{6x^2-17x+12}$

$6x^2 - x - 12$	$2x^2 + 7x + 6$
$6x^2 - 9x + 8x - 12$	$2x^2 + 4x + 3x + 6$
$3x(2x - 3) + 4(2x - 3)$	$2x(x + 2) + 3(x + 2)$
$(3x + 4)(2x - 3)$	$(2x + 3)(x + 2)$
$2x^2 + 11x + 12$	$6x^2 - 17x + 12$
$2x^2 + 8x + 3x + 12$	$6x^2 - 9x - 8x + 12$
$2x(x + 4) + 3(x + 4)$	$3x(2x - 3) - 4(2x - 3)$
$(2x + 3)(x + 4)$	$(3x - 4)(2x - 3)$

$-72 \rightarrow (-9)(8)$

$-9 + 8 \rightarrow -1$

$12 \rightarrow (4)(3)$

$4 + 3 \rightarrow 7$

$24 \rightarrow (8)(3)$

$8 + 3 \rightarrow 11$

$72 \rightarrow (-9)(-8)$

$-9 - 8 \rightarrow -17$

$\dfrac{(3x+4)(2x-3)}{(2x+3)(x+4)} \cdot \dfrac{(2x+3)(x+2)}{(3x-4)(2x-3)}$

$\dfrac{(3x+4)\mathbf{(2x-3)}}{\mathbf{(2x+3)}(x+4)} \cdot \dfrac{\mathbf{(2x+3)}(x+2)}{(3x-4)\mathbf{(2x-3)}}$ Cancel out the bold terms

$\left\{\dfrac{(3x+4)(x+2)}{(x+4)(3x-4)}\right\}$ **or** $\left\{\dfrac{3x^2+10x+8}{3x^2+8x-16}\right\}$

Rational Expressions

For rational expressions, follow these steps when simplifying exercises.

1. If the expression has a division sign, change the division sign to multiplication and flip the second fraction (this can be done when dividing any fraction).
2. Factor all polynomials completely. The four boxes are useful in categorizing the polynomials to factor each one at a time.
3. Once completely factored, cancel out terms that occur in both within any numerator and within any denominator.

When canceling out terms in this matter, the terms (singular and grouped by parenthesis) should be chained together by multiplication. One cannot cancel within the parenthesis and one cannot cancel out terms that are chained by addition or subtraction. To clarify, the addition and subtraction of the two or more terms inside the parenthesis are viewed as a grouped term. This is also used when figuring out the Least Common Denominator (LCD).

Ex 2: Solve:

$$\frac{100}{x^2+6x+9} = \frac{10}{x+3} - \frac{10}{x^2-9}$$

$$\frac{100}{(x+3)(x+3)} = \frac{10}{x+3} - \frac{10}{(x+3)(x-3)} \quad \text{LCD: } (x+3)^2(x-3)$$

$$(x+3)(x+3)(x-3)\left(\frac{100}{(x+3)(x+3)} = \frac{10}{x+3} - \frac{10}{(x+3)(x-3)}\right)$$

$$100(x-3) = 10(x+3)(x-3) - 10(x+3)$$

$$100(x-3) = 10(x^2-9) - 10(x+3)$$

$$100x - 300 = 10x^2 - 90 - 10x - 30$$

$$100x - 300 = 10x^2 - 10x - 120$$

$$10x^2 - 110x + 180 = 0$$

Rational Expressions

Ex 2 (continued): $x^2 - 11x + 18 = 0$ Divide all terms by 10

$$(x - 2)(x - 9) = 0$$

$$x - 2 = 0 \qquad\qquad x - 9 = 0$$

$$x = 2 \qquad\qquad x = 9$$

$$x = \{2, 9\}$$

Within example 2, the LCD was used to eliminate the denominators. This technique was used in previous chapters, but in this case uses grouped terms. When an equal sign is involved with fractions, one can multiply all quantities by the LCD to eliminate the denominators. A short hand notation between the third and fourth steps was used. Essentially, within each fraction, eliminate the denominator and multiply any part(s) of the LCD that were missing from the denominator to the numerator.

Ex 3: Simplify the Complex Fraction:

$$\dfrac{\frac{1}{x+1}+\frac{1}{x+2}}{\frac{1}{x+2}+\frac{1}{x+3}}$$ First, multiply the top and bottom by the LCD.

LCD: $(x + 1)(x + 2)(x + 3)$

$$\left(\dfrac{\frac{1}{x+1}+\frac{1}{x+2}}{\frac{1}{x+2}+\frac{1}{x+3}}\right)\left(\dfrac{(x+1)(x+2)(x+3)}{(x+1)(x+2)(x+3)}\right)$$

$$\dfrac{(x+2)(x+3)+(x+1)(x+3)}{(x+1)(x+3)+(x+1)(x+2)}$$

$$\dfrac{x^2+3x+2x+6+x^2+3x+x+3}{x^2+3x+x+3+x^2+2x+x+2} \rightarrow \left\{\dfrac{2x^2+9x+9}{2x^2+7x+5}\right\}$$

Rational Expressions

Within Intermediate Algebra, this chapter tends to sneak in a new type of word problem that, for this journal, is called Fractional Work.

Ex 4: Gauge, Hunter, and Leni can paint a room when working alone in 3 hours, 4 hours, and 6 hours respectively. How long will it take them to paint the room if they worked together?

Work: Gauge $= \frac{1}{3}$ of the job per hour

Hunter $= \frac{1}{4}$ of the job per hour

Leni $= \frac{1}{6}$ of the job per hour

$\frac{x}{3} + \frac{x}{4} + \frac{x}{6} = 1$ LCD: 12

$12\left(\frac{x}{3}\right) + 12\left(\frac{x}{4}\right) + 12\left(\frac{x}{6}\right) = 12(1)$

$4x + 3x + 2x = 12$

$9x = 12$

$x = \frac{4}{3} \ hours \ or \ 1\frac{1}{3} \ hours$

Solution: **Together they can paint the room in 1 hour and 20 minutes.**

Within Fractional Work word problems, set each person or object applying work as a fraction of how much of the job each can do in one hour. Next, set "x" in the numerators of each fraction rate (this is set as the unknown variable for the total amount of time) and set the sum of all fractions equal to one (or whatever amount of fractional work that is done within the question).

Functions

Primary rule of functions: every x value can only yield one y value.

Secondary rule of functions: treat $f(x)$ as y for solving and simplifying.

<u>Rules for Defining Functions</u>

1. Given Points – x cannot repeat.
2. Given an Equation – y must have an odd power.
3. Given a Graph – Vertical Line Test

In the following examples, which is a function and which is not a function?

Ex 1: $\{(1,2), (2,3), (3,4)\}$ → Function

$\{(1,2), (1,3), (1,4)\}$ → Not a Function

Ex 2: $y^3 = x^4 + 6x^2 - 9$ → Function

$y^2 = x - 4$ → Not a Function

Ex 3:

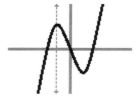

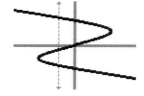

Only crosses once   Crosses more than once

Function   Not a Function

The Vertical Line Test shown in example 3 uses an imaginary vertical line that shifts left to right and counts the number of times the curve of the function is crossed. If the vertical line crosses up to once, then the curve represents a function. If the vertical line crosses more than once, then the curve does not represent a function.

Functions

Notation of Function Groups

1. $f + g \rightarrow f(x) + g(x)$ Addition of two functions
2. $f - g \rightarrow f(x) - g(x)$ Subtraction of two functions
3. $fg \rightarrow f(x)g(x)$ Multiplication of two functions
4. $\dfrac{f}{g} \rightarrow \dfrac{f(x)}{g(x)}$ Division of two functions
5. $f \circ g \rightarrow (f \circ g)(x) \rightarrow f(g(x))$ Composite Functions

The new notation would be the composite function. This notation can be tricky as most students would be unfamiliar to the operator within composite functions. The procedure for composite function is as follows:

Plug in the inner function in for x of the outer function.

Ex 4: Find $(f \circ g)(x)$ when $f(x) = 2x^2 + 4$ and $g(x) = 3x + 5$.

$$f(g(x)) \rightarrow f(3x + 5) \rightarrow 2(3x + 5)^2 + 4$$

$$2(3x + 5)(3x + 5) + 4$$

$$2(9x^2 + 15x + 15x + 25) + 4$$

$$18x^2 + 30x + 30x + 50 + 4$$

$$(f \circ g)(x) = 18x^2 + 60x + 54$$

Variance Equations

1. y varies directly as x: $y = kx$
2. y varies inversely as x: $y = \dfrac{k}{x}$
3. y varies jointly as x and z: $y = kxz$

Domain and Range

Domain – The possible x values of the function. (Leftmost to Rightmost)

Range – The possible y values of the function. (Bottommost to Topmost)

Types of Restrictions on the Domain

1. Variables in the denominator.
2. Variables underneath the radical (square root).
3. Combination of the first two rules.
4. Variables within a logarithmic expression.

Ex 1: $\frac{1}{x-2}$ → $x - 2 \neq 0$ → $x \neq 2$

Domain: $(-\infty, 2) \cup (2, \infty)$

Ex 2: $\sqrt{x+3}$ → $x + 3 \geq 0$ → $x \geq -3$

Domain: $[-3, \infty)$

Ex 3: $\frac{1}{\sqrt{x-4}}$ → $x - 4 > 0$ → $x > 4$

Domain: $(4, \infty)$

Ex 4: $\log(x + 5)$ → $x + 5 > 0$ → $x > -5$

Domain: $(-5, \infty)$

Restrictions on Range can be determined analytically when involving the Inverse Function. The domain of an Inverse Function would be equal to the Range of the original function. (This is used within later Math courses, however.)

Determining Domain and Range visually from graphs: observe the leftmost to rightmost x values, and the bottommost to topmost y values. Breaks within the function can be labeled using the Union notation (∪).

System of Linear Equations

Methods of solving a System of Linear Equations

1. Graphing both linear equations and finding the intersection.
2. Substitution
3. Elimination
4. Method involving three linear equations with three variables.

Ex 1:   Solve the system of equations by graphing:

$$\begin{cases} y = 2x + 4 \\ y = 3x + 3 \end{cases}$$

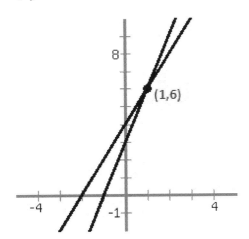

Work:

Solution: $(1, 6)$

System of Linear Equations

Ex 2:   Solve the system of equations by substitution:

$$\begin{cases} 2x + y = 6 \\ 3x + 2y = 8 \end{cases}$$

Work: $2x + y = 6$ $3x + 2(-2x + 6) = 8$ $y = -2x + 6$

          $y = -2x + 6$ $3x - 4x + 12 = 8$ $y = -2(4) + 6$

                                 $-x + 12 = 8$ $y = -8 + 6$

                                 $-x = -4 \rightarrow x = 4$ $y = -2$

Solution: $(\mathbf{4}, -\mathbf{2})$

In example 2, the first step is to select an equation with a variable with an ideal coefficient (either '1' or a value where fractions can be avoided). Otherwise, select either equation and solve for one of the variables. Once the variable is isolated, plug in the resulting expression in for the variable in the other equation and solve for the other variable. As a value is obtained, plug in that value for the respective variable into the isolated variable equation to obtain the other value.

Ex 3:   Solve the system of equations by elimination:

$$\begin{cases} 2x + 3y = 6 \\ 3x + 4y = 12 \end{cases}$$

Work: $\begin{cases} (2x + 3y = 6)(-3) \\ (3x + 4y = 12)(2) \end{cases}$ $2x + 3(-6) = 6$

          $\begin{cases} \mathbf{-6x} - 9y = -18 \\ \mathbf{6x} + 8y = 24 \end{cases}$ $2x - 18 = 6$

          $-y = 6 \rightarrow y = -6$ $2x = 24 \rightarrow x = 12$

Solution: $(\mathbf{12}, -\mathbf{6})$

System of Linear Equation

In example 3 on page 64, select one variable in the system with the lowest LCD between their coefficients. Multiply both sides of each equation in such a way that the selected variables coefficients match the LCD and are opposite in sign. Combine the two new equations to obtain a third equation and isolate the remaining variable. Plug in the resulting value into one of the original equations, and solve for the other variable.

Ex 4: Solve the system of equations:

$$\begin{cases} x + 2y + 3z = 28 \\ 2x + y + 3z = 29 \\ 3x + 2y + z = 32 \end{cases}$$ Label as R1, R2, and R3 respectively.

Work: R1: $(x + 2y + 3z = 28)(-2)$ R1: $(x + 2y + 3z = 28)(-3)$
R2: $2x + y + 3z = 29$ R3: $3x + 2y + z = 32$

R1: $-2x - 4y - 6z = -56$ R1: $-3x - 6y - 9z = -84$
R2: $2x + y + 3z = 29$ R3: $3x + 2y + z = 32$

R4: $-3y - 3z = -27$ R5: $-4y - 8z = -52$

R4: $(-3y - 3z = -27)(-4)$
R5: $(-4y - 8z = -52)(3)$

R4: $12y + 12z = 108$
R5: $-12y - 24z = -156$

R6: $-12z = -48$ → $z = 4$

R4: $-3y - 3(4) = -27$ R1: $x + 2(5) + 3(4) = 28$
$-3y - 12 = -27$ $x + 10 + 12 = 28$
$-3y = -15$ → $y = 5$ $x + 22 = 28$ → $x = 6$

Solution: $(6, 5, 4)$ "(x, y, z)"

System of Linear Equations

In example 4 on page 65, the method is a more complex version of the elimination method. When solving a three equation system, first select one variable to eliminate using two out of the three original equations and use the elimination method. Next, select a new combination of two equations and eliminate the same variable. These calculations will yield two new equations. Select another variable to eliminate from the new equations to solve for the third variable. From there, plug in the known value into one of the two equations with only two variables to obtain another variable value. Finally, plug in the two known variable values into one of the three original equations to obtain the last variable value.

More Word Problem Types

1. Angles: Complementary = $90 - x$; Supplementary = $180 - x$
2. Any level one word problem involving two variables

Ex 5: Find the angle when the sum of its Complementary and Supplementary Angles is 224.

Work: $(90 - x) + (180 - x) = 224$

$270 - 2x = 224$

$-2x = -46$

$x = 23$

Solution: **The angle is 23°**

Author's Note: I will omit examples of the level one word problems with two variables since they are similar to the calculation and set-up as their one variable counterpart. In example 5 on page 41, the volume expression would have been read as "x + y = 20." Therefore, "y = 20 − x."

Inequalities and Absolute Value

Absolute Inequalities

$|x| < c$ $|x| \geq c$

$-c < x < c$ $x \geq c \text{ or } x \leq -c$

Ex 1: $|x - 4| < 6$ Ex 2: $|x - 5| \geq 14$

$-6 < x - 4 < 6$ $x + 5 \geq 14 \text{ or } x + 5 \leq -14$

$-2 < x < 10$ $x \geq 9 \text{ or } x \leq -19$

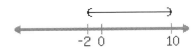   

$\{(-2, 10)\}$ $\{(-\infty, -19] \cup [9, \infty)\}$

Graphing Linear Inequalities

Ex 3:   Graph: $3x + 4y \leq 12$

Work: $3x + 4(0) = 12$

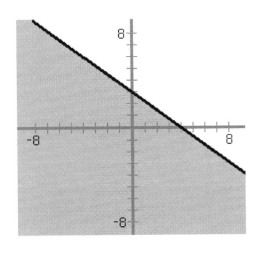

$3x = 12 \rightarrow x = 4 \rightarrow (4,0)$

$3(0) + 4y = 12$

$4y = 12 \rightarrow y = 3 \rightarrow (0,3)$

Test Point: $(0,0)$

$3x + 4y \leq 12$

$3(0) + 4(0) \leq 12$

$0 \leq 12 \rightarrow$ True (Shade the side containing the test point)

Inequalities and Absolute Value

<u>System of Linear Inequalities</u>

Ex 4:   Graph: $\begin{cases} 5x + 6y \leq 30 \\ 4x - 3y \geq 24 \end{cases}$

Work: $5x + 6(0) = 30$ $4x - 3(0) = 24$

$5x = 30 \rightarrow x = 6 \rightarrow (6,0)$ $4x = 24 \rightarrow x = 6 \rightarrow (6,0)$

$5(0) + 6y = 30$ $4(0) - 3y = 24$

$6y = 30 \rightarrow y = 5 \rightarrow (0,5)$ $-3y = 24 \rightarrow y = -8 \rightarrow (0,-8)$

Test Point: $(0,0)$ Test Point: $(0,0)$

$5x + 6y \leq 30$ $4x - 3y \geq 24$

$4(0) - 3(0) \leq 30$ $4(0) - 3(0) \geq 24$

$0 \leq 30 \rightarrow$ True $0 \geq 24 \rightarrow$ False

Solution:

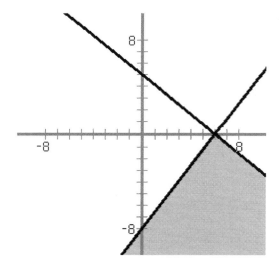

Only the overlap of the two is shaded in the final graph.

Intro to Pre-Calculus

Pre-calculus is a subject within Math that contains advanced algebra. The objective of Pre-calculus is to master algebra before advancing on to Trigonometry and Calculus. In this chapter, I will list the beginning equations within Pre-calculus along with other properties.

Difference Quotient: $\dfrac{f(x+h)-f(x)}{h}, h \neq 0$

Distance: $d = \sqrt{(x_2 - x_1)^2 + (y_2 - y_1)^2}$

Midpoint: $M(x,y) = \left(\dfrac{x_1+x_2}{2}, \dfrac{y_1+y_2}{2}\right)$

Standard Circle: $(x-h)^2 + (y-k)^2 = r^2$

Center: (h,k) Radius $= r$

In the center, h and k both change their signs.

Complete the Square: $\left(\dfrac{b}{2a}\right)^2$ **or** $\left(\dfrac{b}{2}\right)^2$ when $a = 1$ as $ax^2 + bx + c$

Average Rate of Change: $\dfrac{\Delta y}{\Delta x} = \dfrac{f(x_2)-f(x_1)}{x_2-x_1} = \dfrac{y_2-y_1}{x_2-x_1}$

Ex 1:   Solve by completing the square: $x^2 - 4x = 5$

$\left(\dfrac{-4}{2}\right)^2 \rightarrow (-2)^2 \rightarrow 4$ Obtain the ideal value

$x^2 - 4x + \mathbf{4} = 5 + \mathbf{4}$ Add the value to both sides

$x^2 - 4x + 4 = 9$

$(x-2)^2 = 9$ Factor

$\sqrt{(x-2)^2} = \pm\sqrt{9}$ Square root both sides

$x - 2 = \pm 3$

$x - 2 = 3$ $x - 2 = -3$

$x = 5$ $x = -1$

Solution: $x = \{-1, 5\}$

Intro to Pre-Calculus

Symmetry with even and odd functions

1. Plug in "$-x$" into 'x' of $f(x)$
2. Simplify and compare to the original function

   $f(-x) = f(x)$ → Even Function (No signs change in the numerator)

   $f(-x) = -f(x)$ → Odd Function (All signs change in the numerator)
3. Determine symmetry by definition

   Even Function – symmetric to the y-axis

   Odd Function – symmetric to the origin

Multiply by the Conjugate

Ex 2: Simplify: $\dfrac{3+\sqrt{5}}{\sqrt{2}-\sqrt{3}}$

$\left(\dfrac{3+\sqrt{5}}{\sqrt{2}-\sqrt{3}}\right)\left(\dfrac{\sqrt{2}+\sqrt{3}}{\sqrt{2}+\sqrt{3}}\right)$ Multiply top and bottom by the conjugate

$\dfrac{(3+\sqrt{5})(\sqrt{2}+\sqrt{3})}{(\sqrt{2}-\sqrt{3})(\sqrt{2}+\sqrt{3})}$ Rewrite to set up for FOIL method

$\dfrac{3\sqrt{2}+3\sqrt{3}+\sqrt{10}+\sqrt{15}}{\sqrt{4}+\sqrt{6}-\sqrt{6}-\sqrt{9}}$

$\dfrac{3\sqrt{2}+3\sqrt{3}+\sqrt{10}+\sqrt{15}}{2-3}$

$\dfrac{3\sqrt{2}+3\sqrt{3}+\sqrt{10}+\sqrt{15}}{-1}$

$\left\{-3\sqrt{2}-3\sqrt{3}-\sqrt{10}-\sqrt{15}\right\}$

Convert Infinite Decimals to Fractions

Ex 3: $0.555\ldots$

$x = 0.555\ldots$

$10x = 5.555\ldots$

$-x - 0.555\ldots$

$9x = 5$

$x = \dfrac{5}{9}$

Ex 4: $0.2666\ldots$

$x = 0.2666\ldots$

$10x = 2.666\ldots$

$-x - 0.2666\ldots$

$9x = 2.4$

$x = \dfrac{2.4}{9} \rightarrow \dfrac{24}{90} \rightarrow \dfrac{4}{15}$

Ex 5: $0.4545\ldots$

$x = 0.4545\ldots$

$100x = 45.45\ldots$

$-x \ - 0.4545\ldots$

$99x = 45$

$x = \dfrac{45}{99} \rightarrow \dfrac{5}{11}$

Intro to Pre-Calculus

When converting infinite decimals to fractions, first set the infinite decimal equal to x. Multiply both sides by a base power of ten. Subtract both sides by x and the original decimal. This converts the infinite decimal to a finite decimal. Then simplify the result by solving for x and simplifying the fraction.

<u>Simplify Radicals</u>

Ex 6:   Simplify: $48^{\frac{1}{2}} \rightarrow \sqrt{48} \rightarrow \sqrt{16} \cdot \sqrt{3} \rightarrow 4 \cdot \sqrt{3} \rightarrow \{4\sqrt{3}\}$

Ex 7:   Simplify: $54^{\frac{1}{3}} \rightarrow \sqrt[3]{54} \rightarrow \sqrt[3]{27} \cdot \sqrt[3]{2} \rightarrow 3 \cdot \sqrt[3]{2} \rightarrow \{3\sqrt[3]{2}\}$

Radicals are also known as fractional exponents and the number in the upper left corner of the radical represents the value from the denominator in that regards. In figuring out the ideal factors, reference the perfect squares and perfect cubes from the Factoring chapter (Page 54).

Transformation of Functions

Types of Functions

Identity:

$$f(x) = x$$

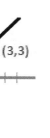

Square:

$$f(x) = x^2$$

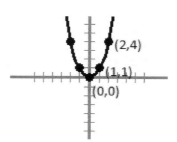

Cube:

$$f(x) = x^3$$

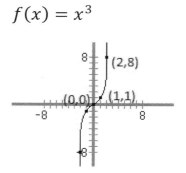

Absolute:

$$f(x) = |x|$$

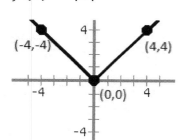

Square root:

$$f(x) = \sqrt{x}$$

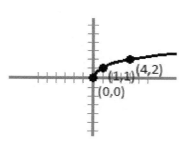

Cube root:

$$f(x) = \sqrt[3]{x}$$

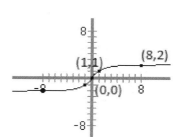

Reciprocal:

$$f(x) = \frac{1}{x}$$

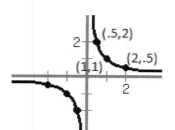

Greatest Common Integer:

$$f(x) = int(x)$$

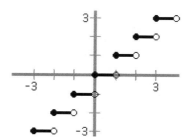

Transformation of Functions

Transformation Rule Set

$$g(x) = af\big(b(x - h)\big) + k$$

a: Vertical Stretch, Shrink, and/or Flip

b: Horizontal Stretch, Shrink, and/or Flip

h: Horizontal Shift – Left (positive) or Right (negative)

k: Vertical Shift – Up (positive) or Down (negative)

Stretch: $|a| > 1$ $|b| < 1$

Shrink: $|a| < 1$ $|b| > 1$

Order of Transformations:

b is applied first. (Divide the x-values of the function by b)

h is applied second.

a is applied third. (Multiply the y-values of the function by a)

k is applied last.

Flip Rule Set:

$f(x) = \sqrt{x}$ $f(x) = \sqrt{-x}$

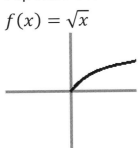 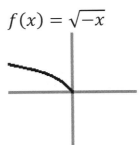

$f(x) = -\sqrt{x}$ $f(x) = -\sqrt{-x}$

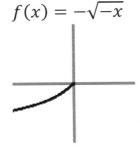

Transformation of Functions

Ex: Graph the following function using transformations:

$$g(x) = 2(x - 4)^2 + 2$$

Work: $y = x^2$ $y = (x - 4)^2$

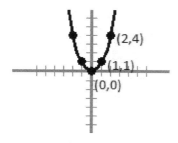

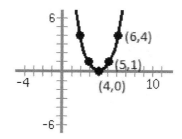

$y = 2(x - 4)^2$ $y = 2(x - 4)^2 + 2$

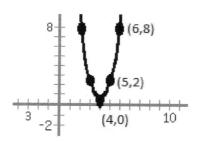

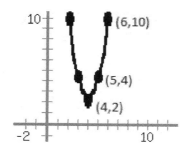

Author's Note: In the example above, I selected one of the unmodified graphs on page 72 as a starting point. The second step is to shift the graph to the right by 4. The third step I multiplied the second steps y-values by 2 to obtain the stretching effect of the function. In the last step, I shifted the graph upward by 2 to obtain the final answer.

Word Problems (Level Two)

Level two word problems involve constructing functions and their equations for use in applications. This type of word problem requires more insight rather than following a common pattern.

Step 1: Analyze and figure out the objective within the application.

Step 2: Reference formulas for the base construction of the equation.

Step 3: Add other data pertaining to the application that was otherwise not included in the function's base design.

Solving the word problem from this point is governed by the data and the function(s) presented in the application.

<u>Types of Objectives (not limited to…)</u>

1. Area and Perimeter
2. Volume and Surface Area
3. Supply and Demand
4. Cost, Revenue, and Profit

<u>Formulas for Area and Perimeter</u>

Square: $A = s^2$ $P = 4s$

Rectangle: $A = lw$ $P = 2l + 2w$

Circle: $A = \pi r^2$ $C = 2\pi r$

Triangle: $A = \frac{1}{2}bh$ $P = a + b + c$

<u>Formulas for Volume and Surface Area</u>

Rectangle Prism (Box): $V = lwh$ $SA = 2lw + 2lh + 2wh$

Sphere: $V = \frac{4}{3}\pi r^3$ $SA = 4\pi r^2$

Cylinder: $V = \pi r^2 h$ $SA = 2\pi r^2 + 2\pi rh$

Word Problems (Level Two)

The other two objective types are related to each other.

Supply and Demand mainly use two linear functions to illustrate the theory. Both tend to be inversely related to one another. These functions do have a base structure as the Cost, Revenue, and Profit functions.

Cost: $C(x) = mx + b$

Revenue: $R(x) = mx$ or $R(x) = px$

Profit: $P(x) = R(x) - C(x)$

Cost, Revenue, and Profit begin as linear functions, but can also appear as quadratic functions as seen in the Quadratic Functions chapter (Page 81, Ex. 5). Constructing the Cost function involves data such as initial costs (b) and item cost (m). The Revenue function can also be constructed in a similar matter, but usually no y intercept or initial revenue is used.

The main theory behind these word problems is to construct complex functions. Commonly such applications require the use of knowledge from composite functions from the Functions chapter (Page 60).

Ex: Express the Volume of an inscribed cylinder of height h and radius r inside a sphere with radius of $R = 4$ in terms of h. (Ref: Pythagorean Theorem Page 90)

Work: First, draw an illustration:

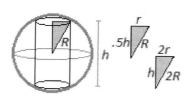

$$a^2 + b^2 = c^2$$
$$(2r)^2 + (h)^2 = (2R)^2$$
$$(2r)^2 + (h)^2 = (2(4))^2$$
$$(2r)^2 + (h)^2 = (8)^2$$
$$4r^2 + h^2 = 64$$
$$4r^2 = 64 - h^2$$
$$r^2 = 16 - \frac{1}{4}h^2$$

$$V = \pi r^2 h$$
$$V = \pi(16 - \frac{1}{4}h^2)h$$
$$\left\{ V = 16\pi h - \frac{\pi}{4}h^3 \right\}$$

Quadratic Functions

Two Forms of Quadratic Equations

$$f(x) = ax^2 + bx + c \qquad\qquad f(x) = a(x-h)^2 + k$$

Vertex: $\quad V_x = -\dfrac{b}{2a}$ $\qquad\qquad$ Vertex: $\quad (h, k)$

$\qquad\qquad V_y = f(V_x)$

When a is positive: The parabola opens upwards. The vertex is the minimum.

When a is negative: The parabola opens downwards. The vertex is the maximum.

Axis of Symmetry: $x = V_x$ $\qquad$ (x value of the vertex)

Solving Quadratic Equations

1. Set the equation equal to zero.
2. If the equation can be factored, then factor and set each grouped term equal to zero and solve for x. If the equation cannot be factored, then use the Quadratic Formula to solve for x.

Quadratic Formula: $\qquad ax^2 + bx + c = 0 \rightarrow x = \dfrac{-b \pm \sqrt{b^2 - 4ac}}{2a}$

Discriminate: $\qquad b^2 - 4ac > 0 \rightarrow$ two real solutions *

$\qquad\qquad\qquad b^2 - 4ac = 0 \rightarrow$ one real solution

$\qquad\qquad\qquad b^2 - 4ac < 0 \rightarrow$ two imaginary solutions

$\quad$ * If $b^2 - 4ac$ results in a perfect square, then the solutions are rational.

Graphing Quadratic Equations

1. Find and plot the vertex.
2. Find two points on one side of the vertex and plot.
3. Reflect those points to the other side via the axis of symmetry.

Quadratic Functions

Ex 1: Graph: $f(x) = 2(x-3)^2 - 4$

Work: Vertex: $(3, -4)$

$$f(4) = 2(4-3)^2 - 4 \rightarrow -2 \quad (4,-2)$$
$$f(5) = 2(5-3)^2 - 4 \rightarrow 4 \quad (5,4)$$

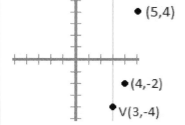 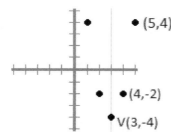 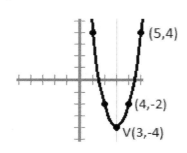

Ex 2: Graph: $f(x) = 2x^2 - 8x + 3$

Work:

$$V_x = -\frac{b}{2a} \rightarrow -\frac{(-8)}{2(2)} \rightarrow 2$$
$$V_y = 2(2)^2 - 8(2) + 3 \rightarrow -5$$

Vertex: $(2, -5)$

$$f(1) = 2(1) - 8(1) + 3 \rightarrow -3 \qquad (1, -3)$$
$$f(0) = 2(0) - 8(0) + 3 \rightarrow 3 \qquad (0,3)$$

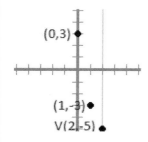 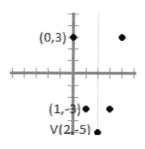 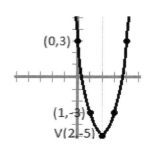

Quadratic Functions

<u>Solving Quadratic Inequalities</u>

1. Change the inequality sign to an equal sign.
2. Set the equation equal to zero.
3. Factor the equation completely.
4. Set each factor equal to zero and solve. The resulting values are known as the critical points of the inequality.
5. Create a table and then select test values within each interval constructed from the critical values from step 4.
6. Check if each test point results in either a positive or negative value.
7. Look back to the original inequality to determine which intervals that satisfy the inequality and contain those intervals as the solution.

Ex 3: Solve the inequality: $x^2 - x - 30 > 0$

Work: $x^2 - x - 30 = 0$

$(x - 6)(x + 5) = 0$ $(x - 6)(x + 5) > 0$

$x - 6 = 0$ $x + 5 = 0$

$x = 6$ $x = -5$ Critical Values: $-5, 6$

	$(-\infty, -5)$	$(-5,6)$	$(6, \infty)$
Test Values	-6	0	8
$x - 6$	$-$	$-$	$+$
$x + 5$	$-$	$+$	$+$
Result	$+$	$-$	$+$

Solution: $(-\infty, -5) \cup (6, \infty)$

Quadratic Functions

Applications involving Quadratic Functions

Ex 4a: A 64 inch wide sheet of metal is to be bent into a rectangular drain (without the top portion) to allow the flow of water. What are the dimmensions of the drain that allows the maximum flow of water?

Work: First, draw an illistration of the application:

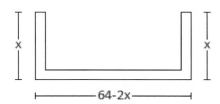

$$A(x) = (64 - 2x)(x)$$
$$A(x) = -2x^2 + 64x$$

Find V_x to obtain one of the dimensions that yields the maximum area.

$$V_x = -\frac{b}{2a} \rightarrow -\frac{(64)}{2(-2)} \rightarrow x = 16$$

$$64 - 2x \rightarrow 64 - 2(16) \rightarrow 32$$

Solution: **The dimensions are 16 inches x 32 inches.**

Ex 4b: What is the maximum area?

$$A(16) = -2(16)^2 + 64(16)$$
$$A(16) = -512 + 1024$$
$$A(16) = 512$$

Solution: **The maximum area is 512 square inches.**

Quadratic Functions

Ex 5: The price function is $p = 0.05x + 1.4$ and the cost function is $C(x) = 0.1x^2 + 0.2x$. Find the number of items (x) to be sold which maximizes the profit, the price in which maximizes the profit, and the maximum profit.

Work:
$$R(x) = px \qquad\qquad \text{Revenue = Price x Items Sold}$$
$$R(x) = (0.05x + 1.4)x$$
$$R(x) = 0.05x^2 + 1.4x$$

$$P(x) = R(x) - C(x)$$
$$P(x) = (0.05x^2 + 1.4x) - (0.1x^2 + 0.2x)$$
$$P(x) = -0.05x^2 + 1.2x$$

$$V_x = -\frac{b}{2a} \rightarrow -\frac{(1.2)}{2(-0.05)} \rightarrow x = 12$$

$$p = 0.05(12) + 1.4$$
$$p = 2.00$$

$$P(12) = -0.05(12)^2 + 1.2(12)$$
$$P(12) = 7.20$$

Solution:
Items sold: **12 items**
Price: **$2.00 per item**
Profit: **$7.20**

Polynomial Functions

Two Forms of Polynomials

      1. $f(x) = Cx^d + \cdots$
      2. $f(x) = C(x - c_1)^d (x - c_2)^d \ldots$

Degree: 1. Degree = d

                   2. Degree = the sum of all d values

End Behavior: $f(x) = \pm Cx^d$ (d is the overall degree)

Turning Points: $TPs = d - 1$ (d is the overall degree)

Multiplicity: The number of times a specific zero occurs.

    Ex 1: $2(x - 3)^4 = 0$
          The zero is 3 with a multiplicity of 4.

    Even Multiplicity: The curve touches and bounces off the x-axis.
    Odd Multiplicity: The curve crosses the x-axis.

Graphing Trends using End Behavior

Even Degree   Odd Degree

$+C$ $-C$ $+C$ $-C$

    This is helpful for estimating graphs which only require the end directions and the number of turning points of the curve.

Asymptotes

Vertical Asymptotes (VA)

 1. Simplify the rational expression in question.
 2. Set each componnent of the denominator equal to zero.
 3. Solve for each to obtain the Vertical Asymptote(s).

Horizontal Asymptotes (HA)

$$f(x) = \frac{cx^a + \cdots}{dx^b + \cdots}$$ "cx^a" and "dx^b" are the leading terms.

 1. $a > b$ No Horizontal Asymptote (Possible Slant Asymptote).
 2. $a = b$ The Horizontal Asymptote is $y = \frac{c}{d}$.
 3. $a < b$ The Horizontal Asymptote is $y = 0$.

Slant Asymptotes (SA)

 If a is just one degree greater than b (Referencing $f(x)$ above), then use synthetic or long division to obtain the Slant Asymptote.

Ex 1: Find all asymptotes: $f(x) = \frac{3x^2 + 4}{2x^2 - 8}$

Work: VA: $2x^2 - 8 = 0$ HA: Since $a = b$
                $2(x^2 - 4) = 0$
                $2(x + 2)(x - 2) = 0$
                $x + 2 = 0$ $x - 2 = 0$

Solution: VA: $\{x = -2, x = 2\}$ HA: $\left\{y = \frac{3}{2}\right\}$

Asymptotes

Ex 2: Find all asymptotes: $f(x) = \frac{x^3 + 5x^2 + 8x + 14}{x^2 - 16}$

Work: VA: $x^2 - 16 = 0$

$(x + 4)(x - 4) = 0$

$x + 4 = 0 \quad x - 4 = 0$

$x = -4 \qquad x = 4$

SA:

$$
\begin{array}{r}
x + 5 \\
x^2 - 16\overline{\smash{\big)}\ x^3 + 5x^2 + 8x + 14} \\
-x^3 \qquad\ \ + 16x \\
\hline
5x^2 + 24x + 14 \\
-5x^2 \qquad + 80 \\
\hline
24x + 94
\end{array}
$$

1. $\frac{x^3}{x^2} \to x$

2. $x(x^2 - 16) \to$

3. $x^3 - 16x$

Solution: VA: $\{x = -4, x = 4\}$ SA: $\{y = x + 5\}$

Long Division Steps:

1. Divide the leading terms of each expression (result on top).
2. Multiply the result of step 1 by the divisor.
3. List the result of step 2 underneath the inside expression.
4. Once underneath, switch the signs of the variables in step 3; combine like terms.
5. Repeat steps 1 through 4 till the leading term inside has a degree that is less than the degree of the devisor.

Polynomial and Rational Expressions

Inequalities

Solving Polynomial or Rational Inequalities has a similar objective as with Quadratic Inequalities. There are more steps to solving Polynomial or Rational Inequalities as opposed to Quadratic Inequalities.

1. Rational Zero Theorem (RZT): List all factors of the coefficients of the leading term and last term, and divide each factor of the last term by each factor of the leading term to yeild the possible rational zeros.
2. Descarte's Rule of Signs: Count the number of sign changes between terms of $f(x)$ and $f(-x)$, which equals the maximum number of positive zeros and negatives zeros respectively.
3. Synthetic Division: Select one of the rational zeros and test using synthetic division. Repeat this step till a quadratic expression is obtained. Rewrite each rational zero as a factor by reversing its sign.
4. Factor the remaining expression.

Ex 1: Solve: $\dfrac{x^3+3x^2-10x-24}{x^3+4x^2-7x-10} \geq 0$

Work: RZT$(x^3 + 3x^2 - 10x - 24)$: $\left(\dfrac{24}{1}\right) \rightarrow \pm 1, \pm 2, \pm 3, \pm 4, \pm 6, \pm 12, \pm 24$

RZT$(x^3 + 4x^2 - 7x - 10)$: $\left(\dfrac{10}{1}\right) \rightarrow \pm 1, \pm 2, \pm 5, \pm 10$

$$\underline{-2}\, \begin{array}{rrrr} 1 & 3 & -10 & -24 \\ & -2 & -2 & 24 \\ \hline 1 & 1 & -12 & 0 \end{array}$$

$$\underline{-5}\, \begin{array}{rrrr} 1 & 4 & -7 & -10 \\ & -5 & 5 & 10 \\ \hline 1 & -1 & -2 & 0 \end{array}$$

$x^2 + x - 12$
$(x + 4)(x - 3)$

$x^2 - x - 2$
$(x - 2)(x + 1)$

$\dfrac{(x+2)(x-3)(x+4)}{(x+1)(x-2)(x+5)} \geq 0$

Polynomial and Rational Expressions

Ex 1 (continued):   Critical values: $-5, -4, -2, -1, 2, 3$

	$(-\infty, -5)$	$(-5, -4]$	$[-4, -2]$	$[-2, -1)$	$(-1, 2)$	$(2, 3]$	$[3, \infty)$
Test	-6	$-\frac{9}{2}$	-3	$-\frac{3}{2}$	0	$\frac{5}{2}$	4
x - 3	−	−	−	−	−	−	+
x - 2	−	−	−	−	−	+	+
x + 1	−	−	−	−	+	+	+
x + 2	−	−	−	+	+	+	+
x + 4	−	−	+	+	+	+	+
x + 5	−	+	+	+	+	+	+
Result	+	−	+	−	+	−	+

Solution: $(-\infty, -5) \cup [-4, -2] \cup (-1, 2) \cup [3, \infty)$

Finding a Function's equation using its zeros

1. Set each zero equal to x.
2. Set each epression in step 1 equal to zero.
3. Rewrite the function as follows: $f(x) = a(x \pm c_1)(x \pm c_2) \dots$
4. Plug in x and y values given to find a.

Ex 2: A function with a degree of 4 has zeros: $2, -3, 4i$ and $f(1) = -204$.

Work: Imaginary and irrational zeros always come in pairs.

$$x = 2 \qquad x = -3 \qquad x = 4i \qquad x = -4i$$
$$x - 2 = 0 \quad x + 3 = 0 \quad x - 4i = 0 \quad x + 4i = 0$$
$$f(x) = a(x - 2)(x + 3)(x - 4i)(x + 4i)$$
$$f(x) = a(x - 2)(x + 3)(x^2 - 16i^2)$$
$$f(x) = a(x - 2)(x + 3)(x^2 + 16)$$
$$-204 = a(1 - 2)(1 + 3)(1 + 16) \rightarrow -204 = -68a \rightarrow a = 3$$
$$f(x) = 3(x - 2)(x + 3)(x^2 + 16)$$
$$f(x) = 3(x^2 + x - 6)(x^2 + 16)$$
$$f(x) = 3(x^4 + x^3 + 10x^2 + 16x - 96)$$

Solution: $\{f(x) = 3x^4 + 3x^3 + 30x^2 + 48x - 288\}$

Exponential and Logarithmic Functions

Converting Forms ("Swing" Method)

$$\log_b c = a \quad \longleftrightarrow \quad c = b^a$$

Transformations of Exponential and Logarithmic Functions

$$f(x) = am^{(b(x-h))} + k \qquad f(x) = a\log_m\big(b(x-h)\big) + k$$

a: Vertical Stretch, Shrink, and/or Flip

b: Horizontal Stretch, Shrink, and/or Flip

h: Horizontal Shift – Left (positive) or Right (negative)

k: Vertical Shift – Up (positive) or Down (negative)

Logarithmic Rules

1. $\log_b 1 = 0$
2. $\log_b b = 1$
3. $b^{\log_b M} = M$
4. $\log_b b^M = M$
5. $\log_b(MN) = \log_b M + \log_b N$
6. $\log_b \left(\dfrac{M}{N}\right) = \log_b M - \log_b N$
7. $\log_b M^r = r\log_b M$
8. $\log_b M = \dfrac{\log_a M}{\log_a b} = \dfrac{\ln M}{\ln b}$

Exponential and Logarithmic Functions

<u>Formulas</u>

1. Compound Interest: $\quad A = P\left(1 + \dfrac{r}{n}\right)^{nt}$

2. Compound Continuously: $\quad A = Pe^{rt}$

3. Growth and Decay: $\quad A(t) = A_0 e^{kt}$

4. Newton's Law of Cooling: $\quad T_f = R + (T_i - R)e^{rt}$

P: Principle or amount invested

A: Final Amount after an interval of time

r: Interest Rate or Cooling Rate

t: Time of investment

n: Number of compounds per year

$A(t)$: Final Amount

A_0: Initial Amount

k: Growth/Decay constant

T_f: Final Temperature

T_i: Initial Temperature

R: Room Temperature

Number of compounds:

"Annually"	$n = 1$
"Semiannually"	$n = 2$
"Quarterly"	$n = 4$
"Monthly"	$n = 12$
"Daily"	$n = 365$

Intro to Trigonometry

Beginning Trigonometric Formulas (θ in radians)

1. Arc Length: $s = r\theta$

2. Area of a sector: $A = \dfrac{1}{2}r^2\theta$

3. Angular Speed: $\omega = \dfrac{\theta}{t}$

4. Linear Speed: $v = r\omega$

Radian and Degree conversion: $180° = \pi$

One Revolution: $360^0 = 2\pi$

Acute Angle: $\theta < 90^0$

Obtuse Angle: $90^0 < \theta < 180°$

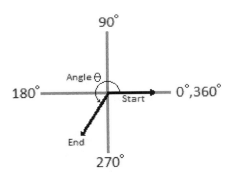

Graphing trigonometric angles starts at the East position (Think in terms of a compass). The angle stops at a specified position based off the position of the four compass directions. Also, the angle rotates Counter-Clockwise when positive and Clockwise when negative.

Intro to Trigonometry

The Right Triangle and the Trigonometric Functions

1. $\sin\theta = \dfrac{opposite}{hypotenuse}$

2. $\cos\theta = \dfrac{adjacent}{hypotenuse}$

3. $\tan\theta = \dfrac{opposite}{adjacent}$

4. $\csc\theta = \dfrac{hypotenuse}{opposite}$

5. $\sec\theta = \dfrac{hypotenuse}{adjacent}$

6. $\cot\theta = \dfrac{adjacent}{opposite}$

One interesting way to remember the trigonometric functions would be:

SOH	CAH	TOA
Sin, Opp, Hyp	Cos, Adj, Hyp	Tan, Opp, Adj

Pythagorean Theorem

$$a^2 + b^2 = c^2$$

a and b: opposite and adjacent sides

c: hypotenuse side

Intro to Trigonometry

Basic Identities

$$\tan\theta = \frac{\sin\theta}{\cos\theta} \qquad \cot\theta = \frac{\cos\theta}{\sin\theta}$$

$$\csc\theta = \frac{1}{\sin\theta} \qquad \sec\theta = \frac{1}{\cos\theta} \qquad \cot\theta = \frac{1}{\tan\theta}$$

$$\sin^2\theta + \cos^2\theta = 1$$

$$\tan^2\theta + 1 = \sec^2\theta$$

$$\cot^2\theta + 1 = \csc^2\theta$$

Side Tricks to the Basic Identities

The last three above can be compressed to remembering only the first equation and alternating that equation into one of the other two.

$$\frac{\sin^2\theta}{\sin^2\theta} + \frac{\cos^2\theta}{\sin^2\theta} = \frac{1}{\sin^2\theta} \rightarrow 1 + \cot^2\theta = \csc^2\theta$$

$$\frac{\sin^2\theta}{\cos^2\theta} + \frac{\cos^2\theta}{\cos^2\theta} = \frac{1}{\cos^2\theta} \rightarrow \tan^2\theta + 1 = \sec^2\theta$$

Other Trigonometric identities are listed in Appendix D.

Finding the Value of Trigonometric Angles

Methods of Finding the Value of Trigonometric Angles

1. Identity Triangles rotated along the x axis and y axis
2. Unit Circle
3. Reference Table with the rule of Trigonometric Signs

Author's Note: There are several methods to obtaining the value of Trigonometric Angles. The issue most students have in this section is mainly due to the various strategies associated within this section. Primarily, the student should experiment with all three methods and select a preferred method that's right for them. Although, mastering more than one method allows the student to have access to back-up strategies during exams.

Identity Triangles (Not Drawn to Scale)

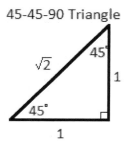

Ex. 1: $\sin 60°$

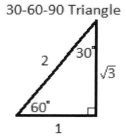

Ex. 2: $\cos 135°$

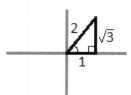

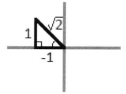

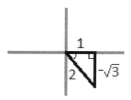

Ex. 3: $\tan 300°$

$$\sin 60° = \frac{\sqrt{3}}{2}$$

$$\cos 135° = \frac{-1}{\sqrt{2}} = -\frac{\sqrt{2}}{2} \qquad \tan 300° = \frac{-\sqrt{3}}{1} = -\sqrt{3}$$

The Identity Triangle is always connected to the center and the x-axis.

Finding the Value of Trigonometric Angles

<u>Unit Circle</u>

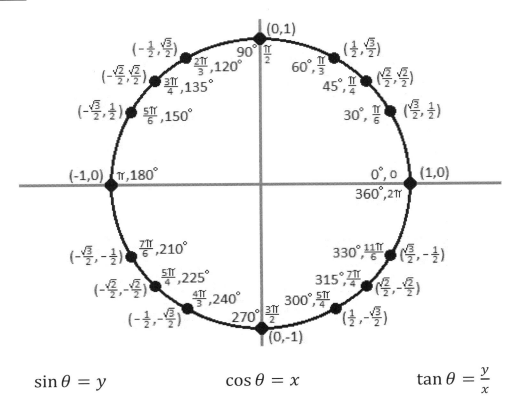

$$\sin \theta = y \qquad \cos \theta = x \qquad \tan \theta = \frac{y}{x}$$

There is a pattern to the values of the points within the Unit Circle. Starting at zero degrees (zero radians), the x-value's numerator decreases from one to zero $(1, \frac{\sqrt{3}}{2}, \frac{\sqrt{2}}{2}, \frac{1}{2}, 0)$ and the y-value's numerator increases from zero to one $(0, \frac{1}{2}, \frac{\sqrt{2}}{2}, \frac{\sqrt{3}}{2}, 1)$. The two groups alternate there patterns every 90 degrees.

Author's Note: I usually tell students to think of one as the square-root of 4 over 2. At that point, the student can think of the numerator as decreasing in sequence from 4 to 0 and increasing in sequence from 0 to 4. This mental visualization may not be compatible for everyone, but it's still an interesting trick.

Finding the Value of Trigonometric Angles

Reference Table

Trig. Values	0°	30°	45°	60°	90°
$\sin\theta$	0	$\frac{1}{2}$	$\frac{\sqrt{2}}{2}$	$\frac{\sqrt{3}}{2}$	1
$\cos\theta$	1	$\frac{\sqrt{3}}{2}$	$\frac{\sqrt{2}}{2}$	$\frac{1}{2}$	0
$\tan\theta$	0	$\frac{\sqrt{3}}{3}$	1	$\sqrt{3}$	Undefined

Reference Angles (RA)

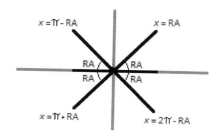

	Find x for $[0,2\pi)$	Find RA
Q1	$x = RA$	$RA = x$
Q2	$x = \pi - RA$	$RA = \pi - x$
Q3	$x = \pi + RA$	$RA = x - \pi$
Q4	$x = 2\pi - RA$	$RA = 2\pi - x$

Rule of Trigonometric Signs

sin csc	All Trig. Values
tan cot	**cos sec**

Positive Trigonometric Values

Q1: All

Q2: $\sin\theta$ and $\csc\theta$

Q3: $\tan\theta$ and $\cot\theta$

Q4: $\cos\theta$ and $\sec\theta$

This method uses a variety of rules, of which can be applied to the other two methods. The table above can be used beyond 90 degrees through the use of Reference Angles and the Rule of Trigonometric Signs. This is done by obtaining the Reference Angle, and then associating that new angle with the table above to obtain the Trigonometric Value. The Rule of Trigonometric Signs can be used to obtain the sign of the Trigonometric Value.

Transformations of Trigonometric Functions

<u>Transformation Rule Set</u>

$$f(x) = A \sin(\omega x - \phi) + k$$

(A) Amplitude = $|A|$

(T) Period = $\frac{2\pi}{\omega}$ ($\sin \theta$, $\cos \theta$, $\csc \theta$, $\sec \theta$) or $\frac{\pi}{\omega}$ ($\tan \theta$, $\cot \theta$)

(PS) Phase Shift = $\frac{\phi}{\omega}$

Vertical Shift = k

Notch Distance = Period $\div$ 4

Amplitude is the vertical height of the Trigonometric function. Period is the horizontal distance the function repeats. The Phase Shift is treated as the starting point (except for $\tan \theta$ where it is treated as the center point). Also, the sine function was used as the core Trigonometric function within the formula above. The other Trigonometric functions can be used in place of the sine function above.

The Procedure for graphing the Trigonometric function is related to Transformations of normal functions. Mainly, for each Period of the Trigonometric function, plot points extended in respect to the Amplitude which produces four intervals that are associated with the pattern of the Trigonometric function.

Transformations of Trigonometric Functions

Default Graphs of the Trigonometric Functions (At least one Period)

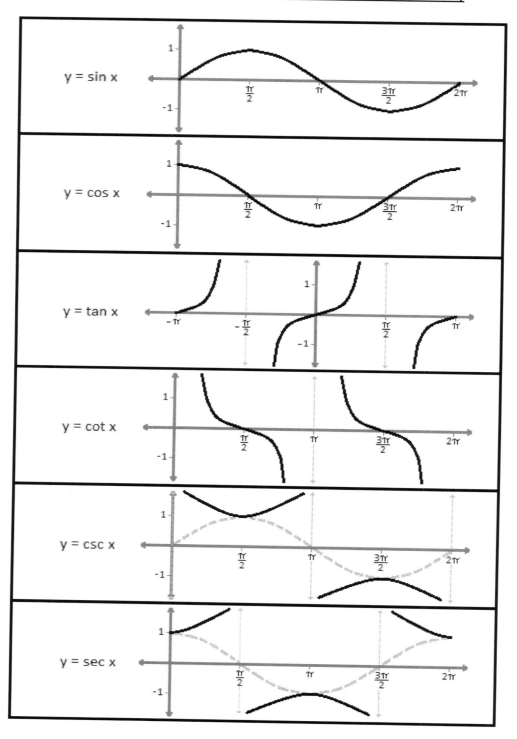

Transformations of Trigonometric Functions

Ex. 1: $y = 2\sin\left(\frac{1}{2}x - \pi\right)$

$A = 2$ $\qquad$ $T = \frac{2\pi}{\frac{1}{2}} \rightarrow 4\pi$ $\qquad$ $PS = \frac{\pi}{\frac{1}{2}} \rightarrow 2\pi$

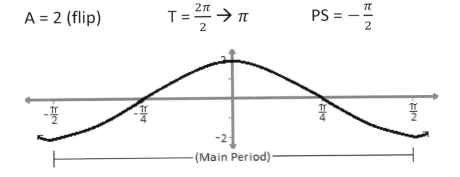

————(Main Period)————

To graph the function above, first plot the starting point that's denoted by the Phase Shift. Next plot the four other points to match the curve of the positive sine function using the notch values (π in this example). Then connect the points with a smooth curve. Add more points based off the sine function pattern till the graph window is filled.

Ex. 2: $y = -2\cos(2x + \pi)$

$A = 2$ (flip) $\qquad$ $T = \frac{2\pi}{2} \rightarrow \pi$ $\qquad$ $PS = -\frac{\pi}{2}$

————(Main Period)————

Trigonometric Proofs

A Trigonometric Proof involves establishing an identity, usually in the form of one Trigonometric equation equals another Trigonometric equation. The main strategy for this type of exercise is as follows:

1. Select the more complex equation of the two (either due to more terms or non-sine/non-cosine equation)
2. Using the Trigonometric Identities to change the selected equation to the terms of sine and cosine.
3. Using Algebraic Techniques to simplify the altered expression to closely resemble the other equation.
4. Using the Trigonometric Identities again to further match the two equations.

The Algebraic Techniques used within Trigonometric Proofs is quite vast. This section will test one's skill and insight greatly. If one practices this section vigorously, one shall be rewarded once one gets to Calculus.

Author's Note: The next page contains only one example of Trigonometric Proofs within this journal. I have optimized the aforementioned example to use various trigonometric identities and various algebraic techniques.

Trigonometric Proofs

Ex: $$\frac{4\left(\cos\theta + \frac{1}{2}\right)^2 - 5}{2\sin 2\theta} = \csc\theta - \tan\theta$$

$$\frac{2\left(\cos\theta + \frac{1}{2}\right)^2 - \frac{5}{2}}{\sin 2\theta} = \csc\theta - \tan\theta$$

$$\frac{2\left(\cos^2\theta + \cos\theta + \frac{1}{4}\right) - \frac{5}{2}}{2\sin\theta\cos\theta} = \csc\theta - \tan\theta$$

$$\frac{2\cos^2\theta + 2\cos\theta + \frac{1}{2} - \frac{5}{2}}{2\sin\theta\cos\theta} = \csc\theta - \tan\theta$$

$$\frac{2\cos^2\theta + 2\cos\theta - 2}{2\sin\theta\cos\theta} = \csc\theta - \tan\theta$$

$$\frac{2(1 - \sin^2\theta) + 2\cos\theta - 2}{2\sin\theta\cos\theta} = \csc\theta - \tan\theta$$

$$\frac{2 - 2\sin^2\theta + 2\cos\theta - 2}{2\sin\theta\cos\theta} = \csc\theta - \tan\theta$$

$$\frac{2\cos\theta - 2\sin^2\theta}{2\sin\theta\cos\theta} = \csc\theta - \tan\theta$$

$$\frac{2\cos\theta}{2\sin\theta\cos\theta} - \frac{2\sin^2\theta}{2\sin\theta\cos\theta} = \csc\theta - \tan\theta$$

$$\frac{1}{\sin\theta} - \frac{\sin\theta}{\cos\theta} = \csc\theta - \tan\theta$$

$$\csc\theta - \tan\theta = \csc\theta - \tan\theta$$

There are many more combinations of Trigonometric Proofs that are possible. Unlike other Math problems, the answer is actually the Proof in its entirety. This exercise is a fine example of why the student must show all his or her work.

Law of Sines, Law of Cosines, and Area of a Triangle using Trigonometry

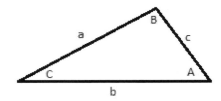

Law of Sines

$$\frac{\sin A}{a} = \frac{\sin B}{b} = \frac{\sin C}{c}$$

Note: Finding any angle through the Law of Sines should be checked by $180° - \theta$ to see if the complement yields a valid second triangle.

Law of Cosines

$$a^2 = b^2 + c^2 - 2bc \cos A$$

$$b^2 = a^2 + c^2 - 2ac \cos B$$

$$c^2 = a^2 + b^2 - 2ab \cos C$$

Area of a Triangle (Using Trigonometry)

$$A = \frac{1}{2} ab \sin C$$

$$A = \frac{1}{2} bc \sin A$$

$$A = \frac{1}{2} ac \sin B$$

$$A = \sqrt{s(s-a)(s-b)(s-c)} \qquad s = \frac{1}{2}(a+b+c)$$

Polar Coordinates and Vector Equations

Rectangular Coordinates: (x, y)

Polar Coordinates: (r, θ) r = radius θ = angle

Convert Rectangular to Polar

$$r = \sqrt{x^2 + y^2} \qquad\qquad \theta = \tan^{-1}\left(\frac{y}{x}\right)$$

Convert Polar to Rectangular

$$x = r \cos \theta \qquad\qquad y = r \sin \theta$$

Vectors

$$\vec{v} = a\hat{\imath} + b\hat{\jmath} \qquad\qquad \|v\| = \sqrt{a^2 + b^2} = \sqrt{x^2 + y^2} = r$$

$$\vec{v} = \|v\| \cos \theta \hat{\imath} + \|v\| \sin \theta \hat{\jmath}$$

Adding two vectors

Let $v_1 = a_1\hat{\imath} + b_1\hat{\jmath}$ and $v_2 = a_2\hat{\imath} + b_2\hat{\jmath}$, then:

$$v_R = (a_1 + a_2)\hat{\imath} + (b_1 + b_2)\hat{\jmath}$$

Dot Product

$$u \cdot v = a_1 a_2 + b_1 b_2$$

Angle between two vectors

$$\cos \theta = \frac{u \cdot v}{\|u\|\|v\|}$$

Polar Coordinates and Vector Equations

Ex. 1: Graph $r = 2 \sin 2\theta$

θ	r	θ	r	θ	r
0	0	$\frac{\pi}{3}$	$\sqrt{3}$	$\frac{3\pi}{4}$	2
$\frac{\pi}{6}$	$\sqrt{3}$	$\frac{\pi}{2}$	0	$\frac{5\pi}{6}$	$-\sqrt{3}$
$\frac{\pi}{4}$	2	$\frac{2\pi}{3}$	$-\sqrt{3}$	π	0

Ex. 2: If an airplane traveling 400 mph in the direction of N60°E suddenly experiences a gust of wind traveling at 80 mph with a direction of S30°E, what would be the airplane's speed and bearings as a result?

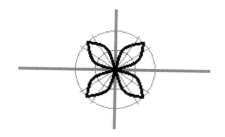

$$v_P = 400 \cos 30° \, \hat{\imath} + 400 \sin 30° \, \hat{\jmath}$$
$$v_P = 200\sqrt{3}\hat{\imath} + 200\hat{\jmath}$$

$$v_w = 80 \cos(-60°)\hat{\imath} + 80 \sin(-60°)\hat{\jmath}$$
$$v_w = 40\,\hat{\imath} + (-40\sqrt{3})\,\hat{\jmath}$$

$$v_R = \left(200\sqrt{3} + 40\right)\hat{\imath} + \left(200 - 40\sqrt{3}\right)\hat{\jmath}$$

$$\|v_R\| = \sqrt{\left(200\sqrt{3} + 40\right)^2 + \left(200 - 40\sqrt{3}\right)^2}$$
$$\|v_R\| \approx 407.92$$

$$\theta = \tan^{-1}\left(\frac{\left(200 - 40\sqrt{3}\right)}{\left(200\sqrt{3} + 40\right)}\right)$$
$$\theta \approx 18.69°$$

Solution: **The airplane is now traveling at 407.92 mph at bearings of N71.31°E.**

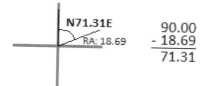

Analytic Geometry

Parabola (Formal)

Equations	Vertex	Focus	Directrix
$(y-k)^2 = \pm 4a(x-h)$	(h,k)	$(h \pm a, k)$	$x = h \mp a$
$(x-h)^2 = \pm 4a(y-k)$	(h,k)	$(h, k \pm a)$	$y = k \mp a$

Ellipse

Equations	Center	Foci	Vertices
$\frac{(x-h)^2}{a^2} + \frac{(y-k)^2}{b^2} = 1$	(h,k)	$(h \pm c, k)$	$(h \pm a, k)$
$\frac{(x-h)^2}{b^2} + \frac{(y-k)^2}{a^2} = 1$	(h,k)	$(h, k \pm c)$	$(h, k \pm a)$

Note: $a > b$ and $c^2 = a^2 - b^2$

Hyperbola

Equations	Center	Foci	Vertices
$\frac{(x-h)^2}{a^2} - \frac{(y-k)^2}{b^2} = 1$	(h,k)	$(h \pm c, k)$	$(h \pm a, k)$
$\frac{(y-k)^2}{b^2} - \frac{(x-h)^2}{a^2} = 1$	(h,k)	$(h, k \pm c)$	$(h, k \pm b)$

Asymptotes: $y - k = \pm \frac{b}{a}(x - h)$

Note: $c^2 = a^2 + b^2$

Analytic Geometry

Ex. 1: Graph the equation: $(y - 3)^2 = 8(x - 2)$

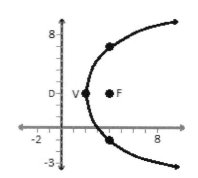

$4a = 8 \rightarrow a = 2 \qquad h = 2 \qquad k = 3$

Vertex: $\quad (h, k) \rightarrow (\mathbf{2, 3})$

Focus: $\quad (h + a, k) \rightarrow (2 + 2, 3) \rightarrow (\mathbf{4, 3})$

Directrix: $\quad x = h - a \rightarrow x = 2 - 2 \rightarrow \mathbf{x = 0}$

     When graphing Parabolas, start by plotting the Vertex. Next, graph the directrix and plot the focus (both must be equidistant in respect to the Vertex). Then from the focus in the perpendicular direction to the vertex, plot two points at a distance equal to double the a-value.

Ex. 2: Graph the equation: $\dfrac{(x-2)^2}{16} + \dfrac{(y+4)^2}{9} = 1$

$a^2 = 16 \rightarrow a = 4 \qquad b^2 = 9 \rightarrow b = 3$

$h = 2 \qquad\qquad\qquad k = -4$

$c^2 = a^2 - b^2 \rightarrow c^2 = 16 - 9 \rightarrow c^2 = 7 \rightarrow c = \sqrt{7}$

Center: $\quad (h, k) \rightarrow (\mathbf{2, -4})$

Vertices: $\quad (h \pm a, k) \rightarrow (2 \pm 4, -4) \rightarrow (\mathbf{-2, -4}), (\mathbf{6, -4})$

Foci: $\quad (h \pm c, k) \rightarrow (2 \pm \sqrt{7}, -4) \rightarrow (\mathbf{2 + \sqrt{7}, -4}), (\mathbf{2 - \sqrt{7}, -4})$

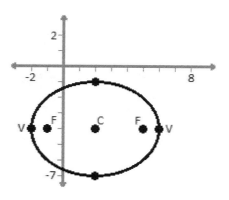

Analytic Geometry

When graphing Ellipses, start by plotting the center. Next, use the a and b values to plot points equal in distance to the a and b values with respect to their matching x or y components.

Ex. 3: $\dfrac{(x-3)^2}{16} - \dfrac{(y-2)^2}{9} = 1$

$\quad\quad a^2 = 16 \rightarrow a = 4 \quad\quad\quad b^2 = 9 \rightarrow b = 3$

$\quad\quad h = 3 \quad\quad\quad\quad\quad\quad\quad k = 2$

$\quad\quad a^2 + b^2 = c^2 \rightarrow 16 + 9 = c^2 \rightarrow c^2 = 25 \rightarrow c = 5$

Center: $\quad (h, k) \rightarrow (\mathbf{3, 2})$

Vertices: $\quad (h \pm a, k) \rightarrow (3 \pm 4, 2) \rightarrow (\mathbf{-1, 2}), (\mathbf{7, 2})$

Foci: $\quad\quad (h \pm c, k) \rightarrow (3 \pm 5, 2) \rightarrow (\mathbf{-2, 2}), (\mathbf{8, 2})$

Asymptotes: $\quad y - 2 = \pm\dfrac{3}{4}(x - 3)$

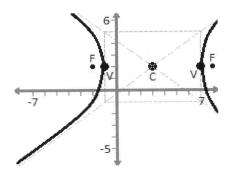

When graphing Hyperbolas, start by plotting the center. Next, use the a and b values to illustrate the x and y distance from the center. Then draw a dashed box showcasing the illustrated points. At this instance, graph two asymptotes crossing the center and the corners of the dashed box. Finally, plot the vertices and use the foci similar to the method involving parabolas to graph the curves.

Sums and Series

Equations of Basic Sums

$$\sum_{k=1}^{n} c = cn \qquad\qquad \sum_{k=1}^{n} k^2 = \frac{n(n+1)(2n+1)}{6}$$

$$\sum_{k=1}^{n} k = \frac{n(n+1)}{2} \qquad\qquad \sum_{k=1}^{n} k^3 = \left[\frac{n(n+1)}{2}\right]^2$$

Arithmetic Sequence and Series (Added/Subtracted Difference)

$a_n = a_1 + (n-1)d$ $\qquad\qquad$ The nth term

$S_n = \frac{n}{2}(a_1 + a_n)$ $\qquad\qquad$ Sum of n terms

Geometric Sequence and Series and Infinite Series (Multiplied Difference)

$a_n = a_1 r^{(n-1)}$ $\qquad\qquad$ The nth term

$S_n = \frac{a_1(1-r^n)}{1-r}$ $\qquad\qquad$ Sum of n terms

$S_\infty = \frac{a_1}{1-r}, |r| < 1$ $\qquad\qquad$ Sum of an infinite series

Binomial Expansion

$$(x + a)^n = \binom{n}{0}x^n + \binom{n}{1}a^1 x^{n-1} + \cdots + \binom{n}{n-1}a^{n-1}x^1 + \binom{n}{n}a^n$$

Note: $\binom{n}{r} = C(n, r)$

Sums and Series

Ex. 1: Find the sum of the first 20 terms of the following series: {4, 7, 10...}

Work: $7 - 4 = 3 \rightarrow d = 3$ Find the d value.

$a_{20} = 4 + (20 - 1)(3) \rightarrow a_{20} = 61$ Find the 20th term.

$S_{20} = \frac{20}{2}(4 + 61) \rightarrow S_{20} = 650$ Find the sum.

Solution: **The sum of the series is 650.**

Ex. 2: Find the 12th term and the sum of the first 15 terms of the following sequence: {3, 6, 12...}

Work: $\frac{6}{3} = 2$ and $\frac{12}{6} = 2 \rightarrow r = 2$ Find the r value.

$a_{12} = (3)(2)^{12-1}$ Find the 12th term.
$a_{12} = (3)(2)^{11}$
$a_{12} = (3)(2048)$
$a_{12} = 6144$

$S_{15} = \frac{(3)(1-2^{15})}{1-2}$ Find the sum of 15 terms.
$S_{15} = \frac{3(1-32768)}{-1}$
$S_{15} = -3(-32767)$
$S_{15} = 98301$

Solution: **The 12th term is 6144 and the sum of the first 15 terms is 98,301.**

Ex. 3: Find the sum of the following infinite series: {192, 96, 48...}

Work: $r = \frac{96}{192} \rightarrow r = \frac{1}{2}$ $S_{\infty} = \frac{192}{1-\frac{1}{2}} \rightarrow S_{\infty} = \frac{192}{\frac{1}{2}} \rightarrow S_{\infty} = 384$

Solution: **The sum of the infinite series is 384.**

Matrices

Types of Matrix Exercises

    1. Adding and Subtracting Matrices

    2. Multiplying Matrices

    3. System of Equations (Matrix Form)

    4. Inverse

    5. Simplex Method

    6. Generations

Adding and Subtracting Matrices requires all matrices involved to be the same dimensions (same number of rows and columns between all matrices).

Ex. 1: $\begin{bmatrix} 4 & 5 \\ 6 & 7 \end{bmatrix} + \begin{bmatrix} 8 & 7 \\ 6 & 5 \end{bmatrix} - \begin{bmatrix} 5 & 4 \\ 3 & 2 \end{bmatrix}$

$$\begin{bmatrix} 4+8-5 & 5+7-4 \\ 6+6-3 & 7+5-2 \end{bmatrix} \rightarrow \begin{bmatrix} \mathbf{7} & \mathbf{8} \\ \mathbf{9} & \mathbf{10} \end{bmatrix}$$

Multiplying Matrices requires the number of columns on the left matrix to match the number of rows on the right matrix. Then multiply the matrices by the left matrix's rows by the right matrix's columns. (Remember: Row by Column!)

Ex. 2: $\begin{bmatrix} 3 & 5 \\ 7 & 9 \end{bmatrix} \begin{bmatrix} 4 & 6 \\ 8 & 10 \end{bmatrix}$

$$\begin{bmatrix} (3)(4)+(5)(8) & (3)(6)+(5)(10) \\ (7)(4)+(9)(8) & (7)(6)+(9)(10) \end{bmatrix} \rightarrow \begin{bmatrix} \mathbf{52} & \mathbf{68} \\ \mathbf{100} & \mathbf{132} \end{bmatrix}$$

Ex. 3: $\begin{bmatrix} 1 & 2 & 3 \\ 4 & 5 & 6 \end{bmatrix} \begin{bmatrix} 7 & 8 \\ 9 & 10 \\ 11 & 12 \end{bmatrix}$

$$\begin{bmatrix} (1)(7)+(2)(9)+(3)(11) & (1)(8)+(2)(10)+(3)(12) \\ (4)(7)+(5)(9)+(6)(11) & (4)(8)+(5)(10)+(6)(12) \end{bmatrix} \rightarrow$$

$$\begin{bmatrix} \mathbf{58} & \mathbf{64} \\ \mathbf{139} & \mathbf{154} \end{bmatrix}$$

Matrices

Solving a System of Equations in the form of a matrix requires row manipulation in such a way that all that remains in each row would be just one variable equal to a value. There is a pattern to this procedure in the form of a "staircase" of ones and zeros:

$$\begin{array}{ccc} x & y & z \\ \end{array}$$

$$\left[\begin{array}{ccc|c} 1^{①} & 0 & 0 & \sim \\ 0^{②} & 1^{④} & 0 & \sim \\ 0^{③} & 0^{⑤} & 1^{⑥} & \sim \end{array}\right]$$

The target values for steps 1-6 are shown above. The last three zeros can be obtained in any order once the "staircase" is formed. When one reaches the final matrix from above, one can label all values for all variables.

Row Manipulation instructions (should be done one at a time):
to obtain a one, multiply that respective row by the target's reciprocal;
to obtain a zero, add or subtract the target row by the row which has a one in the same column, multiply the second row by the targets opposite value;
switching rows can be done at any time for this type of matrix.

Ex. 4: $\begin{cases} 2x + 3y + z = 17 \\ x - 2y + 4z = 12 \\ 3x + y - 2z = 1 \end{cases} \rightarrow$

$$\left[\begin{array}{ccc|c} ② & 3 & 1 & 17 \\ 1 & -2 & 4 & 12 \\ 3 & 1 & -2 & 1 \end{array}\right] \quad \text{(Switch Rows)} \quad \begin{array}{c} R1 \curvearrowright R2 \end{array} \longrightarrow \left[\begin{array}{ccc|c} 1 & -2 & 4 & 12 \\ ② & 3 & 1 & 17 \\ 3 & 1 & -2 & 1 \end{array}\right]$$

$$\begin{array}{l} R2: \ \ 2 \ \ 3 \ \ 1 \ \ 17 \\ \underline{-2R1: -2 \ \ 4 \ -8 \ -24} \\ \ \ \ \ \ \ \ 0 \ \ 7 \ -7 \ \ -7 \\ \\ R2 - 2R1 = R2(New) \end{array} \longrightarrow$$

$$\left[\begin{array}{ccc|c} 1 & -2 & 4 & 12 \\ 0 & 7 & -7 & -7 \\ ③ & 1 & -2 & 1 \end{array}\right] \quad \begin{array}{l} R3: \ \ 3 \ \ 1 \ \ -2 \ \ \ 1 \\ \underline{-3R1: -3 \ \ 6 \ -12 \ -36} \\ \ \ \ \ \ \ \ 0 \ \ 7 \ -14 \ -35 \\ \\ R3 - 3R1 = R3(New) \end{array} \longrightarrow \left[\begin{array}{ccc|c} 1 & -2 & 4 & 12 \\ 0 & ⑦ & -7 & -7 \\ 0 & 7 & -14 & -35 \end{array}\right] \quad \begin{array}{c} \frac{1}{7}R2 \end{array} \longrightarrow$$

Matrices

Ex. 4 continued:

$$\begin{bmatrix} 1 & -2 & 4 & | & 12 \\ 0 & 1 & -1 & | & -1 \\ 0 & 7 & -14 & | & -35 \end{bmatrix}$$

R3: 0 7 -14 -35
-7R2: 0 -7 7 7
⎯⎯⎯⎯⎯⎯⎯⎯⎯⎯
    0 0 -7 -28

R3 - 7R2 = R3(New) →

$$\begin{bmatrix} 1 & -2 & 4 & | & 12 \\ 0 & 1 & -1 & | & -1 \\ 0 & 0 & -7 & | & -28 \end{bmatrix}$$

$-\frac{1}{7}R3$ →

$$\begin{bmatrix} 1 & -2 & 4 & | & 12 \\ 0 & 1 & -1 & | & -1 \\ 0 & 0 & 1 & | & 4 \end{bmatrix}$$

R2: 0 1 -1 -1
R3: 0 0 1 4
⎯⎯⎯⎯⎯⎯⎯⎯
    0 1 0 3

R2 + R3 = R2(New) →

$$\begin{bmatrix} 1 & -2 & 4 & | & 12 \\ 0 & 1 & 0 & | & 3 \\ 0 & 0 & 1 & | & 4 \end{bmatrix}$$

R1: 1 -2 4 12
2R2: 0 2 0 6
-4R3: 0 0 -4 -16
⎯⎯⎯⎯⎯⎯⎯⎯⎯⎯
    1 0 0 2

R1 + 2R2 - 4R3 = R1(New) →

$$\begin{bmatrix} 1 & 0 & 0 & | & 2 \\ 0 & 1 & 0 & | & 3 \\ 0 & 0 & 1 & | & 4 \end{bmatrix}$$

Solution: **x = 2, y = 3, z = 4**

Finding the inverse of the Matrix is similar to the previous type. Next to the matrix, add another matrix connected to the original matrix with the same dimensions but has a diagonal set of ones and zeros surrounding it. Then, solve the original matrix and the result on the other side is the inverse. (One cannot switch rows using this procedure.)

Ex. 5: $\begin{bmatrix} 2 & 3 & 1 \\ 3 & 1 & 2 \\ 1 & 2 & 3 \end{bmatrix}^{-1}$

$$\left[\begin{array}{ccc|ccc} 2 & 3 & 1 & 1 & 0 & 0 \\ 3 & 1 & 2 & 0 & 1 & 0 \\ 1 & 2 & 3 & 0 & 0 & 1 \end{array}\right]$$

$\frac{1}{2}R1$ →

$$\left[\begin{array}{ccc|ccc} 1 & \frac{3}{2} & \frac{1}{2} & \frac{1}{2} & 0 & 0 \\ 3 & 1 & 2 & 0 & 1 & 0 \\ 1 & 2 & 3 & 0 & 0 & 1 \end{array}\right]$$

R2 - 3R1 →

Matrices

Ex. 5 continued:

$$\left[\begin{array}{ccc|ccc} 1 & \frac{3}{2} & \frac{1}{2} & \frac{1}{2} & 0 & 0 \\ 0 & -\frac{7}{2} & \frac{1}{2} & -\frac{3}{2} & 1 & 0 \\ ①& 2 & 3 & 0 & 0 & 1 \end{array}\right] \xrightarrow{R3 - R1} \left[\begin{array}{ccc|ccc} 1 & \frac{3}{2} & \frac{1}{2} & \frac{1}{2} & 0 & 0 \\ 0 & \boxed{-\frac{7}{2}} & \frac{1}{2} & -\frac{3}{2} & 1 & 0 \\ 0 & \frac{1}{2} & \frac{5}{2} & -\frac{1}{2} & 0 & 1 \end{array}\right] \xrightarrow{-\frac{2}{7}R2}$$

$$\left[\begin{array}{ccc|ccc} 1 & \frac{3}{2} & \frac{1}{2} & \frac{1}{2} & 0 & 0 \\ 0 & 1 & -\frac{1}{7} & \frac{3}{7} & -\frac{2}{7} & 0 \\ 0 & \boxed{\frac{1}{2}} & \frac{5}{2} & -\frac{1}{2} & 0 & 1 \end{array}\right] \xrightarrow{R3 - \frac{1}{2}R2} \left[\begin{array}{ccc|ccc} 1 & \frac{3}{2} & \frac{1}{2} & \frac{1}{2} & 0 & 0 \\ 0 & 1 & -\frac{1}{7} & \frac{3}{7} & -\frac{2}{7} & 0 \\ 0 & 0 & \boxed{\frac{18}{7}} & -\frac{5}{7} & \frac{1}{7} & 1 \end{array}\right] \xrightarrow{\frac{7}{18}R3}$$

$$\left[\begin{array}{ccc|ccc} 1 & \frac{3}{2} & \frac{1}{2} & \frac{1}{2} & 0 & 0 \\ 0 & 1 & \boxed{-\frac{1}{7}} & \frac{3}{7} & -\frac{2}{7} & 0 \\ 0 & 0 & 1 & -\frac{5}{18} & \frac{1}{18} & \frac{7}{18} \end{array}\right] \xrightarrow{R2 + \frac{1}{7}R3} \left[\begin{array}{ccc|ccc} 1 & \boxed{\frac{3}{2}} & \boxed{\frac{1}{2}} & \frac{1}{2} & 0 & 0 \\ 0 & 1 & 0 & \frac{7}{18} & -\frac{5}{18} & \frac{1}{18} \\ 0 & 0 & 1 & -\frac{5}{18} & \frac{1}{18} & \frac{7}{18} \end{array}\right] \xrightarrow[R1 - \frac{1}{2}R3]{R1 - \frac{3}{2}R2}$$

$$\left[\begin{array}{ccc|ccc} 1 & 0 & 0 & \frac{1}{18} & \frac{7}{18} & -\frac{5}{18} \\ 0 & 1 & 0 & \frac{7}{18} & -\frac{5}{18} & \frac{1}{18} \\ 0 & 0 & 1 & -\frac{5}{18} & \frac{1}{18} & \frac{7}{18} \end{array}\right]$$

Solution: $\begin{bmatrix} 2 & 3 & 1 \\ 3 & 1 & 2 \\ 1 & 2 & 3 \end{bmatrix}^{-1} = \begin{bmatrix} \frac{1}{18} & \frac{7}{18} & -\frac{5}{18} \\ \frac{7}{18} & -\frac{5}{18} & \frac{1}{18} \\ -\frac{5}{18} & \frac{1}{18} & \frac{7}{18} \end{bmatrix}$

Matrices

Simplex Method

Simplex Method (or Tableu) is also similar to Type 3. The main difference would be that this matrix involves systems of inequalities and an objective function. These exercises in particular take a while to complete in comparison to the other exercises in this chapter.

1. Construct the Simplex
2. Select the Pivot Point
3. Manipulate the Target Column
4. Repeat steps 2 and 3 if needed

Ex. 6: Casey wishes to create nut mixes for a fundraiser. She has 800 ounces of peanuts, 1000 ounces of cashews, and 600 ounces of pecans. Mixture 1 requires 6 ounces of peanuts, 4 ounces of cashews, and 2 ounces of pecans and yields a profit of $1.50. Mixture 2 requires 4 ounces of peanuts, 6 ounces of cashews, and 2 ounces of pecans and yields a profit of $1.75. Mixture 3 requires 2 ounces of peanuts, 4 ounces of cashews, and 6 ounces of pecans and yields a profit of $2.00. How many of each nut mix must she create to maximize profit?

Intro: Let x = the number of mixture 1

Let y = the number of mixture 2

Let z = the number of mixture 3

Data:

	x	y	z		Max
Peanuts	6	4	2	$\leq$	800
Cashews	4	6	4	$\leq$	1000
Pecans	2	2	6	$\leq$	600
Objective	1.5	1.75	2	=	M

To contruct the Simplex, the columns will be all unknowns from the data, a number of "slack" variables equal to the number of inequalitites within the

Matrices

Simplex Method

system, a variable M for maximum, and the restriction of the inequalities. The number of rows equals the number of inequalities plus the objective equation.

$$
\begin{array}{ccccccc|c}
x & y & z & s1 & s2 & s3 & M & \\
6 & 4 & 2 & 1 & 0 & 0 & 0 & 800 \\
4 & 6 & 4 & 0 & 1 & 0 & 0 & 1000 \\
2 & 2 & 6 & 0 & 0 & 1 & 0 & 600 \\
\hline
-1.5 & -1.75 & -2 & 0 & 0 & 0 & 1 & 0
\end{array}
$$

Notice that the last row went through a signs change, and within the slack variables and M variable there is a placeholder pattern of the "staircase."

The Pivot Point (Element) is selected in two steps: 1) the column with the strongest negative in the last row, 2) the row with the lowest, non-negative, ratio between the last column values and the elements in the selected column from the previous step.

$$
\begin{array}{ccccccc|c}
x & y & z & s1 & s2 & s3 & M & \\
6 & 4 & 2 & 1 & 0 & 0 & 0 & 800 \\
4 & 6 & 4 & 0 & 1 & 0 & 0 & 1000 \\
2 & 2 & ⑥ & 0 & 0 & 1 & 0 & 600 \\
\hline
-1.5 & -1.75 & -2 & 0 & 0 & 0 & 1 & 0
\end{array}
$$

$\frac{800}{2} = 400$

$\frac{1000}{4} = 250$

$\frac{600}{6} = 100$ ◄

Lowest Ratio

Strongest Negative

Once the Pivot Point is set, use row manipulation in order to change it to a one. With it, continue to use row manipulation to change the other elements inside the column containing the Pivot Point to zeros.

Matrices

Simplex Method

Ex. 6 continued:

x	y	z	s1	s2	s3	M	
6	4	2	1	0	0	0	800
4	6	4	0	1	0	0	1000
2	2	⑥	0	0	1	0	600
-1.5	-1.75	-2	0	0	0	1	0

$\frac{1}{6}R3$ →

x	y	z	s1	s2	s3	M	
6	4	②	1	0	0	0	800
4	6	4	0	1	0	0	1000
$\frac{1}{3}$	$\frac{1}{3}$	1	0	0	$\frac{1}{6}$	0	100
-1.5	-1.75	-2	0	0	0	1	0

$R1 - 2R3$ →

x	y	z	s1	s2	s3	M	
$\frac{16}{3}$	$\frac{10}{3}$	0	1	0	$-\frac{1}{3}$	0	600
4	6	④	0	1	0	0	1000
$\frac{1}{3}$	$\frac{1}{3}$	1	0	0	$\frac{1}{6}$	0	100
-1.5	-1.75	-2	0	0	0	1	0

$R2 - 4R3$ →

x	y	z	s1	s2	s3	M	
$\frac{16}{3}$	$\frac{10}{3}$	0	1	0	$-\frac{1}{3}$	0	600
$\frac{8}{3}$	$\frac{14}{3}$	0	0	1	$-\frac{2}{3}$	0	600
$\frac{1}{3}$	$\frac{1}{3}$	1	0	0	$\frac{1}{6}$	0	100
-1.5	-1.75	(-2)	0	0	0	1	0

$R4 + 2R3$ →

x	y	z	s1	s2	s3	M	
$\frac{16}{3}$	$\frac{10}{3}$	0	1	0	$-\frac{1}{3}$	0	600
$\frac{8}{3}$	$\frac{14}{3}$	0	0	1	$-\frac{2}{3}$	0	600
$\frac{1}{3}$	$\frac{1}{3}$	1	0	0	$\frac{1}{6}$	0	100
$-\frac{5}{6}$	$-\frac{13}{12}$	0	0	0	$\frac{1}{3}$	1	200

$\frac{600}{10/3} = 180$

$\frac{600}{14/3} = \frac{900}{7}$ ◄

$\frac{100}{1/3} = 300$

$\frac{3}{14}R2$ →

Matrices

Simplex Method

Ex. 6 continued:

$$\left[\begin{array}{ccccccc|c}
\frac{16}{3} & \left(\frac{10}{3}\right) & 0 & 1 & 0 & -\frac{1}{3} & 0 & 600 \\
\frac{4}{7} & 1 & 0 & 0 & \frac{3}{14} & -\frac{1}{7} & 0 & \frac{900}{7} \\
\frac{1}{3} & \frac{1}{3} & 1 & 0 & 0 & \frac{1}{6} & 0 & 100 \\
\hline
-\frac{5}{6} & -\frac{13}{12} & 0 & 0 & 0 & \frac{1}{3} & 1 & 200
\end{array}\right]$$

$R1 - \frac{10}{3}R2 \longrightarrow$

$$\left[\begin{array}{ccccccc|c}
\frac{24}{7} & 0 & 0 & 1 & -\frac{5}{7} & \frac{1}{7} & 0 & \frac{1200}{7} \\
\frac{4}{7} & 1 & 0 & 0 & \frac{3}{14} & -\frac{1}{7} & 0 & \frac{900}{7} \\
\frac{1}{3} & \left(\frac{1}{3}\right) & 1 & 0 & 0 & \frac{1}{6} & 0 & 100 \\
\hline
-\frac{5}{6} & -\frac{13}{12} & 0 & 0 & 0 & \frac{1}{3} & 1 & 200
\end{array}\right]$$

$R3 - \frac{1}{3}R2 \longrightarrow$

$$\left[\begin{array}{ccccccc|c}
\frac{24}{7} & 0 & 0 & 1 & -\frac{5}{7} & \frac{1}{7} & 0 & \frac{1200}{7} \\
\frac{4}{7} & 1 & 0 & 0 & \frac{3}{14} & -\frac{1}{7} & 0 & \frac{900}{7} \\
\frac{1}{7} & 0 & 1 & 0 & -\frac{1}{14} & \frac{3}{14} & 0 & \frac{400}{7} \\
\hline
-\frac{5}{6} & \left(-\frac{13}{12}\right) & 0 & 0 & 0 & \frac{1}{3} & 1 & 200
\end{array}\right]$$

$R4 + \frac{13}{12}R2 \longrightarrow$

$$\left[\begin{array}{ccccccc|c}
\left(\frac{24}{7}\right) & 0 & 0 & 1 & -\frac{5}{7} & \frac{1}{7} & 0 & \frac{1200}{7} \\
\frac{4}{7} & 1 & 0 & 0 & \frac{3}{14} & -\frac{1}{7} & 0 & \frac{900}{7} \\
\frac{1}{7} & 0 & 1 & 0 & -\frac{1}{14} & \frac{3}{14} & 0 & \frac{400}{7} \\
\hline
-\frac{3}{14} & 0 & 0 & 0 & \frac{13}{56} & \frac{15}{84} & 1 & \frac{2375}{7}
\end{array}\right]$$

$\dfrac{1200/7}{24/7} = 50$ ◄

$\dfrac{900/7}{4/7} = 225$

$\dfrac{400/7}{1/7} = 400$

$\frac{7}{24}R1 \longrightarrow$

$$\left[\begin{array}{ccccccc|c}
1 & 0 & 0 & \frac{7}{24} & -\frac{5}{24} & \frac{1}{24} & 0 & 50 \\
\left(\frac{4}{7}\right) & 1 & 0 & 0 & \frac{3}{14} & -\frac{1}{7} & 0 & \frac{900}{7} \\
\frac{1}{7} & 0 & 1 & 0 & -\frac{1}{14} & \frac{3}{14} & 0 & \frac{400}{7} \\
\hline
-\frac{3}{14} & 0 & 0 & 0 & \frac{13}{56} & \frac{15}{84} & 1 & \frac{2375}{7}
\end{array}\right]$$

$R2 - \frac{4}{7}R1 \longrightarrow$

Matrices

Simplex Method

Ex. 6 continued:

$$
\left[
\begin{array}{ccccccc|c}
1 & 0 & 0 & \frac{7}{24} & -\frac{5}{24} & \frac{1}{24} & 0 & 50 \\
0 & 1 & 0 & -\frac{1}{6} & \frac{1}{3} & -\frac{1}{6} & 0 & 100 \\
\boxed{\frac{1}{7}} & 0 & 1 & 0 & -\frac{1}{14} & \frac{3}{14} & 0 & \frac{400}{7} \\
\hline
-\frac{3}{14} & 0 & 0 & 0 & \frac{13}{56} & \frac{15}{84} & 1 & \frac{2375}{7}
\end{array}
\right]
\quad \xrightarrow{\ R3 - \frac{1}{7}R1\ }
$$

$$
\left[
\begin{array}{ccccccc|c}
1 & 0 & 0 & \frac{7}{24} & -\frac{5}{24} & \frac{1}{24} & 0 & 50 \\
0 & 1 & 0 & -\frac{1}{6} & \frac{1}{3} & -\frac{1}{6} & 0 & 100 \\
0 & 0 & 1 & -\frac{1}{24} & -\frac{1}{24} & \frac{5}{24} & 0 & 50 \\
\hline
\boxed{-\frac{3}{14}} & 0 & 0 & 0 & \frac{13}{56} & \frac{15}{84} & 1 & \frac{2375}{7}
\end{array}
\right]
\quad \xrightarrow{\ R4 + \frac{3}{14}R1\ }
$$

$$
\left[
\begin{array}{ccccccc|c}
1 & 0 & 0 & \frac{7}{24} & -\frac{5}{24} & \frac{1}{24} & 0 & 50 \\
0 & 1 & 0 & -\frac{1}{6} & \frac{1}{3} & -\frac{1}{6} & 0 & 100 \\
0 & 0 & 1 & -\frac{1}{24} & -\frac{1}{24} & \frac{5}{24} & 0 & 50 \\
\hline
0 & 0 & 0 & \frac{1}{16} & \frac{3}{16} & \frac{3}{16} & 1 & 350
\end{array}
\right]
$$

Force the fraction crazy columns equal to zero.

$x = 50$, $y = 100$, $z = 50$, $s_1 = 0$, $s_2 = 0$, $s_3 = 0$, $M = 350$

Solution: **To maximize profit, Casey would have to create 50 of Mixture 1, 100 of Mixture 2, and 50 of Mixture 3. The maximum profit would be $350.**

Matrices

Generation Matrices are sets of matrices that observe percentage transition within a system between iterations.

Ex. 7: A chest contains three candy flavors: cherry, blue berry, and chocolate. The probabilities of the candy the Children pick are as follows: If the first pick is cherry, then the next pick would be 40% cherry, 25% blue berry, and 35% chocolate; If the first pick is blue berry, then the next pick would be 20% cherry, 45% blue berry, and 35% chocolate; If the first pick is chocolate, then the next would be 25% cherry, 20% blue berry, and 55% chocolate. When the candy is first selected, 30% picked cherry, 30% picked blue berry, and 40% picked chocolate. What are the selected percentages after one, two, three, and infinite selections?

Intro: Constructed Matrix of the selection process for each generation.
Let A = cherry, B = blue berry, and C = chocolate.

$$
\begin{array}{c}
\text{First Pick} \\
\begin{array}{ccc}
A & B & C
\end{array} \\
\text{Second Pick} \quad
\begin{array}{c}
A \\ B \\ C
\end{array}
\left[
\begin{array}{ccc}
0.40 & 0.20 & 0.25 \\
0.25 & 0.45 & 0.20 \\
0.35 & 0.35 & 0.55
\end{array}
\right]
\end{array}
$$

Next, construct the initial percentage of selection.

$$
\begin{array}{c}
A \\ B \\ C
\end{array}
\left[
\begin{array}{c}
0.30 \\
0.30 \\
0.40
\end{array}
\right]
$$

Work: Multiply the generation matrix by the initial matrix equal to the number of iterations.

Matrices

Ex. 7 continued:

First Iteration

$$\begin{bmatrix} 0.40 & 0.20 & 0.25 \\ 0.25 & 0.45 & 0.20 \\ 0.35 & 0.35 & 0.55 \end{bmatrix} \begin{bmatrix} 0.30 \\ 0.30 \\ 0.40 \end{bmatrix} \rightarrow \begin{bmatrix} 0.28 \\ 0.29 \\ 0.43 \end{bmatrix}$$

Solution 1   **2nd Pick: 28% cherry, 29% blue berry, and 43% chocolate.**

Second Iteration

$$\begin{bmatrix} 0.40 & 0.20 & 0.25 \\ 0.25 & 0.45 & 0.20 \\ 0.35 & 0.35 & 0.55 \end{bmatrix} \begin{bmatrix} 0.28 \\ 0.29 \\ 0.43 \end{bmatrix} \rightarrow \begin{bmatrix} 0.2775 \\ 0.2865 \\ 0.4360 \end{bmatrix}$$

Soultion 2   **3rd Pick: 27.75% cherry, 28.65% blue berry, 43.6% chocolate.**

Third Iteration

$$\begin{bmatrix} 0.40 & 0.20 & 0.25 \\ 0.25 & 0.45 & 0.20 \\ 0.35 & 0.35 & 0.55 \end{bmatrix} \begin{bmatrix} 0.2775 \\ 0.2865 \\ 0.4360 \end{bmatrix} \rightarrow \begin{bmatrix} 0.2773 \\ 0.2855 \\ 0.4372 \end{bmatrix}$$

Solution 3   **4th Pick: 27.73% cherry, 28.55% blue berry, 43.72% chocolate.**

For infinite iterations, one can take the generation matrix to a high power (At around a power of 10 should be fine, but only advisable if one has a graphing calculator) or do iterations until one is satified with the result (when the result stops changing significantly).

Matrices

Ex. 7 continued:

Fourth Iteration

$$\begin{bmatrix} 0.40 & 0.20 & 0.25 \\ 0.25 & 0.45 & 0.20 \\ 0.35 & 0.35 & 0.55 \end{bmatrix} \begin{bmatrix} 0.2773 \\ 0.2855 \\ 0.4372 \end{bmatrix} \rightarrow \begin{bmatrix} 0.2773 \\ 0.2852 \\ 0.4375 \end{bmatrix}$$

Many Iterations (In calculator)

$$\begin{bmatrix} 0.40 & 0.20 & 0.25 \\ 0.25 & 0.45 & 0.20 \\ 0.35 & 0.35 & 0.55 \end{bmatrix}^{10} \begin{bmatrix} 0.30 \\ 0.30 \\ 0.40 \end{bmatrix} \rightarrow \begin{bmatrix} 0.2773 \\ 0.2852 \\ 0.4375 \end{bmatrix}$$

Solution 4   **Many picks: 27.73% cherry, 28.52% blue berry, 43.75% chocolate.**

Exercise 7 could also be displayed in the following arrangment.

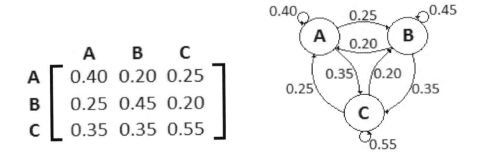

$$\begin{array}{c} \\ A \\ B \\ C \end{array} \begin{array}{ccc} A & B & C \\ \begin{bmatrix} 0.40 & 0.20 & 0.25 \\ 0.25 & 0.45 & 0.20 \\ 0.35 & 0.35 & 0.55 \end{bmatrix} \end{array}$$

The above orientation is helpful for organizing the data.

Linear Programming

Linear programming involves several linear inequalities into one system. The approach is the same as with linear inequalities, but the graphing portion tends to be different depending on the professor's or teacher's preference. Although, most follow the theme of shading the eliminated sections instead of the solution due to the higher number of inequalities. Once a feasible solution is obtained, list the vertices of the feasible solution. Then plug those values into the objective function, and the solution would be either the maximum or the minimum value depending on which the exercise has requested.

Ex. 1:   Maximize $4x + 7y$ subject to

$$\begin{cases} 3x + y \geq 12 \\ x + y \leq 8 \\ x + 4y \geq 12 \\ x \geq 0 \\ y \geq 0 \end{cases}$$

Work:

$3x + y = 12$ $x + y = 8$ $x + 4y = 12$

$y = -3x + 12$ $y = -x + 8$ $(0) + 4y = 12$

$y = 3 \rightarrow (0,3)$

$x + 4(0) = 12$

$x = 12 \rightarrow (12,0)$

Test $(0,0)$:

$3x + y \geq 12 \rightarrow 0 \geq 12$

False

$x + y \leq 8 \rightarrow 0 \leq 8$

True

$x + 4y \geq 12 \rightarrow 0 \geq 12$

False

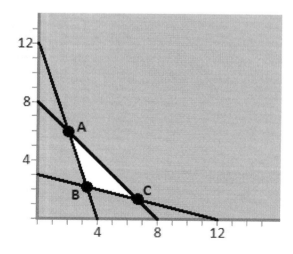

Linear Programming

Ex. 1 continued:

Vertices:

$$A = \begin{cases} 3x + y = 12 \\ x + y = 8 \end{cases} \qquad B = \begin{cases} 3x + y = 12 \\ x + 4y = 12 \end{cases} \qquad C = \begin{cases} x + y = 8 \\ x + 4y = 12 \end{cases}$$

$3x + (-x + 8) = 12$ $\qquad$ $x + 4(-3x + 12) = 12$ $\qquad$ $x + 4(-x + 8) = 12$

$2x = 4$ $\qquad\qquad\qquad$ $-11x = -36$ $\qquad\qquad\quad$ $-3x = -20$

$x = 2$ $\qquad\qquad\qquad\quad$ $x = \dfrac{36}{11}$ $\qquad\qquad\qquad$ $x = \dfrac{20}{3}$

$y = -(2) + 8$ $\qquad\qquad$ $y = -3\left(\dfrac{36}{11}\right) + 12$ $\qquad$ $y = -\left(\dfrac{20}{3}\right) + 8$

$y = 6$ $\qquad\qquad\qquad\quad$ $y = \dfrac{24}{11}$ $\qquad\qquad\qquad$ $y = \dfrac{4}{3}$

$A(2,6)$ $\qquad\qquad\qquad$ $B\left(\dfrac{36}{11}, \dfrac{24}{11}\right)$ $\qquad\qquad$ $C\left(\dfrac{20}{3}, \dfrac{4}{3}\right)$

Objective Function:

$M = 4x + 7y$

$M = 4(2) + 7(6) \rightarrow M = 8 + 42 \rightarrow M = 50$ (Maximum Value)

$M = 4\left(\dfrac{36}{11}\right) + 7\left(\dfrac{24}{11}\right) \rightarrow M = \dfrac{144}{11} + \dfrac{168}{11} \rightarrow M = \dfrac{312}{11} \rightarrow M \approx 28.36$

$M = 4\left(\dfrac{20}{3}\right) + 7\left(\dfrac{4}{3}\right) \rightarrow M = \dfrac{80}{3} + \dfrac{28}{3} \rightarrow M = \dfrac{108}{3} \rightarrow M = 36$

Solution: **A Max of 50 is obtained when x = 2 and y = 6.**

Probability

Brief Explanation on Venn Diagrams and Sets

<u>Venn Diagrams</u>

1. Two Set Venn Diagram
2. Three Set Venn Diagram

Ex. 1: A survey involving 100 students were asked about which classes they were taking for the next semester. The results of the survey: 45 are taking Math, 41 are taking Chemistry, 34 are taking Physics, 13 are taking Math and Chemistry, 10 are taking Math and Physics, 12 are taking Chemistry and Physics, and 5 are taking all three classes. Complete a Venn Diagram and answer the following questions:

a. How many students are taking Math or Chemistry?

b. How many students are taking at least two of these classes?

c. How many students are not taking any of the three classes?

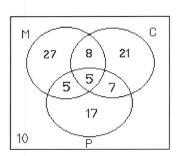

a. $n(M \cup C) = 27 + 8 + 21 + 5 + 5 + 7 = $ **73**

b. $8 + 5 + 5 + 7 = $ **25**

c. $n((M \cup C \cup P)') = $ **10**

The process in Example 1 requires one to work from the "inside out." Start by labeling the center value as 5. Next, obtain the three "leaf" values by taking the difference between the center value and the value from each of the intersections between two sets ($13 - 5 = 8$, $10 - 5 = 5$, $12 - 5 = 7$). Then obtain the values of the remaining part of each circle by taking the difference between the set value and the center values ($45 - 8 - 5 - 5 = 27$, $41 - 8 - 5 - 7 = 21$, $34 - 5 - 5 - 7 = 17$). Finally, obtain the outer most value by subtracting all the circle values from the total ($100 - 27 - 8 - 21 - 5 - 5 - 7 - 17 = 10$).

Probability

Brief Explanation on Venn Diagrams and Sets

Sets and Symbols

1. Union (∪)   Combination of Both Sets
2. Intersection (∩)   Overlap or Common Elements of Both Sets
3. Complement (A')   Inverted Set

A ∪ B   A ∩ B   (A ∪ B)'

      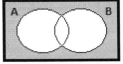

Ex. 2: Let A = {a, b, c, d}, B = {c, d, e, f}, and U = {a, b, c, d, e, f}
Find A ∪ B, A ∩ B, and A'.

A ∪ B → {a, b, c, d} ∪ {c, d, e, f} → **{a, b, c, d, e, f}**

A ∩ B → {a, b, c, d} ∩ {c, d, e, f} → **{c, d}**

A' → {a, b, c, d}' → **{e, f}**

Number of Subsets Equation

Number of Subsets within the set = 2^N

N = number of elements within the set

Ex. 3: How many subsets are in the set {a, b, c, d, e, f, g, h}?

2^N → $2^{(8)}$ → **256 subsets**

Probability

Common Types of Basic Probability

1. Binary System
2. Unordered Selection
3. Ordered Selection
4. Conditional
5. Baye's Theorem
6. Complex Binary
7. Subtypes: Single/Multiple, Events/Squences

Author's Note: Probability is a tricky subject. The wording and approach of probability exercises can differ between each other, yet can appear to have the same objective. Ultimately, insight is greatly needed as probability senerios can get very complex and intense. Practice this section vigorously.

Binary System: Events that have two outcomes. Total outcomes = 2^N

Ex. 4: Flip 8 coins. Find the probability of obtaining 5 heads?

Notation: Pr(5H) → Out of 8 flips, choose 5 heads to appear:

$$\frac{C(8,5)}{2^8} \to \frac{56}{256} \to \left\{\frac{7}{32}\right\}$$

Ex. 5: A test contains 16 true or false questions. Find the probability of answering 12 or more of the questions correctly.

Notation: $Pr(X \geq 12)$ → Pr(12) + Pr(13) + Pr(14) + Pr(15) + Pr(16)

$$\frac{C(16,12)}{2^{16}} + \frac{C(16,13)}{2^{16}} + \frac{C(16,14)}{2^{16}} + \frac{C(16,15)}{2^{16}} + \frac{C(16,16)}{2^{16}} \to$$

$$\frac{1820}{65536} + \frac{560}{65536} + \frac{120}{65536} + \frac{16}{65536} + \frac{1}{65536} \to \left\{\frac{2517}{65536}\right\}$$

Probability

Unordered and Ordered Selection

When order does not matter: $C(n,r)$ Combination
When order does matter: $P(n,r)$ Permutations

Ex. 6: There are 9 boys (Gauge, Hunter, Levi, Cody, Kevin, Mason, Wyatt, Logan, and Stefin) and 3 girls (Casey, Leni, Madison). Find the probability of the following situations:

Ex. 6a: I select 4 children from the group randomly. What is the probability of selecting 3 boys and 1 girl?

$$\frac{C(9,3) \cdot C(3,1)}{C(12,4)} \rightarrow \frac{84 \cdot 3}{495} \rightarrow \frac{252}{495} \rightarrow \left\{\frac{28}{55}\right\}$$

The above first step reads "out of 9 boys, choose 3; out of 3 girls, choose 1; over out of 12 children, choose 4 total."

Ex. 6b: I select two children. What is the probability of selecting Leni and Casey, in that order?

$$\frac{1}{12} \cdot \frac{1}{11} \rightarrow \left\{\frac{1}{132}\right\}$$

Ex. 6c: I select 6 children. What is the probability of selecting at least 2 girls?

2 Events are possible: Pr(2 girls) and Pr(3 girls) → Pr(2) + Pr(3) →

$$\frac{C(9,4) \cdot C(3,2)}{C(12,6)} + \frac{C(9,3) \cdot C(3,3)}{C(12,6)} \rightarrow \frac{126 \cdot 3}{924} + \frac{84 \cdot 1}{924} \rightarrow \frac{462}{924} \rightarrow \left\{\frac{1}{2}\right\}$$

Probability

Ex. 6d: I select 5 children. What is the probability of selecting at least 2 boys?

4 Events are possible: Pr(2 boys) + Pr(3 boys) + Pr(4 boys) + Pr(5 boys)

$$\frac{C(9,2) \cdot C(3,3)}{C(12,5)} + \frac{C(9,3) \cdot C(3,2)}{C(12,5)} + \frac{C(9,4) \cdot C(3,1)}{C(12,5)} + \frac{C(9,5) \cdot C(3,0)}{C(12,5)}$$

$$\frac{36 \cdot 1}{792} + \frac{84 \cdot 3}{792} + \frac{126 \cdot 3}{792} + \frac{126 \cdot 1}{792}$$

$$\frac{36}{792} + \frac{252}{792} + \frac{378}{792} + \frac{126}{792} \rightarrow \frac{792}{792} \rightarrow \{1\}$$

Ex. 6e: use the complement of the probability for exercise 6d above.

$$1 - Pr(1 \text{ or less boys}) \rightarrow 1 - Pr(4 \text{ or } 5 \text{ girls}) \rightarrow 1 - 0 \rightarrow \{1\}$$

The Probability of selecting 4 or more girls is not possible since there are only 3 girls within Exercise 6.

Author's Note: Use of the complement is very useful in calculating probability. Often, thinking about the probability of an event not occuring tends to give us insight into the problem at hand. This is evident in Example 9b and 9c on page 128.

Probability

<u>Conditional Probability</u>

$$Pr(E|F) = \frac{Pr(E\cap F)}{Pr(F)}$$ Probability of E given F.

Ex. 7: A child has a 25% chance of having blonde hair and has a 6.25% chance of having blonde hair and green eyes. What is the probability of the child having green eyes given that the child has blonde hair?

Find Pr(Green Eyes | Blonde Hair)

Ex. 7 continued:

Pr(Blonde) = 0.25   Pr(Green Eyes and Blonde Hair) = 0.0625

Pr(Green Eyes | Blonde Hair) = Pr(Green Eyes and Blonde Hair) / Pr(Blonde)

Pr(Green Eyes | Blonde Hair) = 0.0625 / 0.25 → **{0.25}**

<u>Baye's Theorem</u>

$$Pr(B|A) = \frac{Pr(A|B)Pr(B)}{Pr(A|B)Pr(B)+Pr(A|B')Pr(B')}$$

Ex. 8: A child has a 30% chance if having blonde hair. The probability the child has green eyes given he/she has blonde hair is 5%. The probability the child has green eyes given he/she does not have blonde hair is 35%. Find the probability of the child having blonde hair given he/she has green eyes?

Let A = Green Eyes and B = Blonde Hair.

$$Pr(B|A) = \frac{Pr(A|B)Pr(B)}{Pr(A|B)Pr(B)+Pr(A|B')Pr(B')} \rightarrow \frac{(0.05)(0.30)}{(0.05)(0.30)+(0.35)(0.70)} \rightarrow \frac{0.015}{0.260} \rightarrow \left\{\frac{3}{52}\right\}$$

Probability

Complex Binomial (Binomial Theorem)

$$Pr(x = k) = C(n, k)p^k q^{n-k} \qquad q = 1 - p$$

n = number of trials   p = probability of success
k = number of successes   q = probability of failure

Ex. 9: There is a 10 question mulitple choice test. Probability of guessing the right answer is 0.2 (5 possible answers per question). Find the following probabilities:

Ex. 9a: Probability of getting 9 or more correct.

Pr(x ≥ 9) →
Pr(x = 9) + Pr(x = 10) →
$C(10,9)(0.2)^9(0.8)^1 + C(10,10)(0.2)^{10}(0.8)^0$ →
$0.000004096 + 0.0000001024$ →{**0. 0000041984**}

Ex. 9b: Probability of getting at least 2 correct.

Pr(x ≥ 2) → 1 − Pr(x ≤ 1) →
1 − Pr(x = 0) − Pr(x = 1) →
$1 - C(10,0)(0.2)^0(0.8)^{10} + C(10,1)(0.2)^1(0.8)^9$ →
$1 - 0.1073741824 - 0.268435456$ →
{**0. 624190**} Rounded to 6 decimal places.

Ex. 9c: Probability of getting at most 7 correct.

Pr(x ≤ 7) → 1 − Pr(x ≥ 8) →
1 −(Pr(x = 8) + Pr(x = 9) + Pr(x = 10)) →
$1 - (C(10,8)(0.2)^8(0.8)^2 + C(10,9)(0.2)^9(0.8)^1 + C(10,10)(0.2)^{10}(0.8)^0)$ →
$1 - 0.000073728 - 0.000004096 - 0.0000001024$ →
{**0. 999922**} Rounded to 6 decimal places

Basic Statistics

Common Types

1. Z-table and Bell Curve (normal distribution)
2. Binomial Approximation
3. Confidence Interval

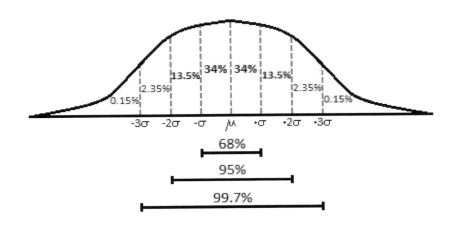

Z-Table and Bell Curve (normal distribution)

The Z-table in the Appendix of this journal is used to refence the z-values after using this equation (μ: mean and σ: standard deviation):

$$Z = \frac{X - \mu}{\sigma}$$

There are three scnerios of calculations involving this equation and the Z-table. All three share the same procedure of using the equation above to obtain the Z-value. Use the Z-value with the Z-table (Appendix B) to obtain the probability of the area shaded to the left, and apply the appropriate calculation depending on the situation involved.

Shading to the left: $\Pr(Z \leq b)$ → Prob. $= p$
Shading to the right: $\Pr(Z \geq b)$ → Prob. $= 1 - p$
Shading between two values: $\Pr(a \leq Z \leq b)$ → Prob. $= p_b - p_a$

Basic Statistics

Ex. 1: Find the probability of X being less than 14 while the mean is 10 and the standard deviation is 5.

Work: $\Pr(X \leq 14)$ $\mu = 10$ $\sigma = 5$

$Z = \frac{14-10}{5} \rightarrow Z = 0.8$

$\Pr(Z \leq 0.8)$

0.8

{**0.7881**}

Ex. 2: Find the probability of X being greater than 18 while the mean is 24 and the standard deviation is 3.

Work: $\Pr(X \geq 18)$ $\mu = 24$ $\sigma = 3$

$Z = \frac{18-24}{3} \rightarrow Z = -2$

$\Pr(Z \geq -2)$

-2

$1 - 0.0228 \rightarrow$ {**0.9772**}

Ex. 3: Find the probability of X being in between 12 and 16 while the mean is 20 and the standard deviation is 4.

Work: $\Pr(12 \leq X \leq 16)$ $\mu = 20$ $\sigma = 4$

$Z = \frac{12-20}{4} \rightarrow Z = -2$ $Z = \frac{16-20}{4} \rightarrow Z = -1$

$\Pr(-2 \leq Z \leq -1)$

-2 -1

$0.1587 - 0.0228 \rightarrow$ {**0.1359**}

Basic Statistics

Binomial Approximation

$$\mu = np \qquad\qquad \sigma = \sqrt{npq} \qquad\qquad q = 1 - p$$

Ex. 4: Hunter has a probability of 0.125 for hitting a homerun. If he has 64 at bats in a session, what's the overall probability that he will hit 6 or more homeruns?

Work: Given: $n = 64$ $p = 0.125$ $q = 0.875$
$\mu = (64)(0.125) \rightarrow \mu = 8$
$\sigma = \sqrt{(64)(0.125)(0.875)} \rightarrow \sigma = 2.6458$
$\Pr(X \geq 6)$

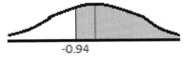

Include a half unit into the shaded portion.
$\Pr(X \geq 5.5)$ This is to compansate for binomial approximation.
$Z = \frac{5.5 - 8}{2.6458} \rightarrow Z = -0.94$
$\Pr(Z \geq -0.94)$ Reference the closest value on the table.

-0.94

$1 - 0.1711 \rightarrow \{\mathbf{0.8289}\}$

More precise values for probability can be obtained through more detailed tables.

Confidence Interval

$$\bar{x} \pm Z^* \frac{s}{\sqrt{n}} \qquad\qquad \text{Margin of Error: } Z^* \frac{s}{\sqrt{n}}$$

Cofidence Level	Z^*		
80%	1.283	$\bar{x}$:	sample mean
90%	1.645	s:	sample std. deviation
95%	1.96	n:	sample size
99%	2.576		

Finance

Compound Interest (Reference: Exponential and Logarithmic Functions)

$$A = P\left(1 + \frac{r}{n}\right)^{nt} \qquad\qquad A = Pe^{rt}$$

"Annually"	$n = 1$	P: Principle or amount invested
"Semiannually"	$n = 2$	A: Final Amount after an amount of time
"Quarterly"	$n = 4$	r: Interest Rate
"Monthly"	$n = 12$	t: Time of investment
"Daily"	$n = 365$	n: Number of compounds per year

Credit Cards and Installments

$$ADB = \frac{a_1\, d_1 + a_2\, d_2 + \cdots + a_n\, d_n}{Cycle} \qquad MFC = (ADB)\left(\frac{r}{365}\right)(Cycle)$$

a_i: Balance for the period

d_i: Days within the period

r: Interest Rate (APR: Annual Percentage Rate)

ADB: Average Daily Balance

MFC: Monthly Finance Charge

$Cycle$: Days within the billing cycle which is governed by the initial month.

    31 days: Jan, Mar, May, Jul, Aug, Oct, and Dec

    30 days: Apr, Jun, Sep, Nov

    28 days: Feb (29 days if the exercise declares a leap year)

$d_i = end\ date - start\ date$

$d_i = cycle + end\ date - start\ date$ If the month changes

$d_i = cycle - [sum\ of\ other\ periods]$ If last period in cycle

Finance

Ex. 1: Find the Average Daily Balance, Monthly Finance Charge, and new Balance after the cycle for a credit card with a starting billing cycle on October 8th, APR of 6.5%, initial balance of $120.00, and has the following transactions:

October 12th:	$24.83 charge
October 15th:	$60.00 payment
October 21th:	$37.82 charge
November 2nd:	$25.81 charge

Date	Balance	Period	Calculations	
Oct 8	120.00	4	120.00 + 24.83 = 144.83	12 – 8 = 4
Oct 12	144.83	3	144.83 – 60.00 = 84.83	15 – 12 = 3
Oct 15	84.83	6	84.83 + 37.82 = 122.65	21 – 15 = 6
Oct 21	122.65	12	122.65 + 25.81 = 148.46	33 – 21 = 12
Nov 2	148.46	6		31 –25 = 6

$$ADB = \frac{(120.00)(4)+(144.83)(3)+(84.83)(6)+(122.65)(12)+(148.46)(6)}{31} \rightarrow \{\$\mathbf{122.13}\}$$

$$MFC = (122.13)\left(\frac{0.065}{365}\right)(31) \rightarrow \{\$\mathbf{0.67}\}$$

New Balance: $148.46 + 0.67 \rightarrow \{\$\mathbf{149.13}\}$

The New Balance is equal to the sum of the last balance in the cycle and the Monthly Finance Charge.

Finance

<u>Annuities and Mortgages</u>

$$FV = P\left[\frac{\left(1+\frac{r}{n}\right)^{nt}-1}{\frac{r}{n}}\right] \qquad PV = P\left[\frac{1-\left(1+\frac{r}{n}\right)^{-nt}}{\frac{r}{n}}\right]$$

Future Value (Annuities)　　　　　Present Value (Mortgages)

P: Monthly (Periodic) Investment or Payment

r: rate (APR)

t: time (in years)

n: number of periods per year (Commonly: $n = 12$)

Ex. 2: If $1000 is deposited monthly into an annuity that pays 8.5% compounded monthly, how much would it accumulate to after 20 years?

$$P = 1000 \quad r = 0.085 \quad t = 20 \qquad n = 12$$

$$FV = (1000)\left[\frac{\left(1+\frac{0.085}{12}\right)^{(12)(20)}-1}{\frac{0.085}{12}}\right] \rightarrow \{\$626,988.95\}$$

Ex. 3: How much would someone have to invest monthly into an annuity paying 6.5% to earn $100,000 in 10 years?

$$FV = 100,000 \qquad r = 0.065 \quad t = 10 \qquad n = 12$$

$$FV = P\left[\frac{\left(1+\frac{r}{n}\right)^{nt}-1}{\frac{r}{n}}\right] \rightarrow P = FV\left[\frac{\frac{r}{n}}{\left(1+\frac{r}{n}\right)^{nt}-1}\right] \rightarrow$$

$$P = (100000)\left[\frac{\frac{0.065}{12}}{\left(1+\frac{0.065}{12}\right)^{(12)(10)}-1}\right] \rightarrow \{\$593.81\}$$

Finance

Ex. 4a: You and your family are thinking of buying a $95,000 house at an interest rate of 3.6% compounded monthly and amortized (length of mortgage) over 30 years. What will be the monthly payment and how much interest will be paid over the 30 year loan?

$$PV = 95{,}000 \qquad r = 0.036 \quad t = 30 \qquad n = 12$$

$$PV = P\left[\frac{1-\left(1+\frac{r}{n}\right)^{-nt}}{\frac{r}{n}}\right] \rightarrow P = PV\left[\frac{\frac{r}{n}}{1-\left(1+\frac{r}{n}\right)^{-nt}}\right] \rightarrow$$

$$P = (95000)\left[\frac{\frac{0.036}{12}}{1-\left(1+\frac{0.036}{12}\right)^{-(12)(30)}}\right] \rightarrow \{\$431.91\}$$

Total of Loan: $431.91 * 12 * 30 \rightarrow$ $155,487.60

Interest Paid: $155,487.60 − $95,000

$$\{\$60{,}487.60\}$$

Ex. 4b: How much will you still owe after 5, 10, and 20 years?

$t = 25$ (After 5 years)

$$PV = (431.91)\left[\frac{1-\left(1+\frac{0.036}{12}\right)^{-(12)(25)}}{\frac{0.036}{12}}\right] \rightarrow \{\$85{,}357.25\}$$

$t = 20$ (After 10 years)

$$PV = (431.91)\left[\frac{1-\left(1+\frac{0.036}{12}\right)^{-(12)(20)}}{\frac{0.036}{12}}\right] \rightarrow \{\$73{,}816.70\}$$

$t = 10$ (After 20 years)

$$PV = (431.91)\left[\frac{1-\left(1+\frac{0.036}{12}\right)^{-(12)(10)}}{\frac{0.036}{12}}\right] \rightarrow \{\$43{,}471.39\}$$

Limits

Author's Note: the first subject within Calculus involves Limits. I decided not to include an intro chapter as there would be no extra information to add onto the previous concepts. Keep in mind: Calculus does require mastery of Algebra and Trigonometry.

Limit Definition

The value the function is targeting while approaching the declared x-value.

Procedure

1. Plug in x directly if possible. (Cannot yield a result of undefined)
2. Reduce the expression using the methods discussed in previous chapters. (The part of the expression that is canceled out is also called the removable discontinuity.)
3. Find the limit by using a table of values which progressively gets closer to the target. Or, find the limit by using the graph of the function.
4. If all the above are inconclusive, then use limit theorems.

Formal Definition of a Limit (Epsilon-Delta Method)

$$\lim_{x \to c} f(x) = L \qquad |x - c| < \sigma \qquad |f(x) - L| < \varepsilon$$

This method involves a proof to be established. Essentially, take the $|f(x) - L| < \varepsilon$ expression to mimic the $|x - c| < \sigma$ expression. The theory and concept would yield the following: if ε and σ vary directly (Variance on page 61), then the effects of change of range and domain between them would be affected in the same matter. This would in essence narrow the range and domain towards the target value.

Author's Note: There are other procedures of the epsilon-delta method. Primarily, students should focus on the method his or her professor implements.

Limits

Ex. 1: $\lim\limits_{x \to 4} x^2 + 5 = 21$

Work: $|x - 4| < \sigma$ $\qquad |(x^2 + 5) - 21| < \varepsilon$

$|x^2 - 16| < \varepsilon \to |(x + 4)(x - 4)| < \varepsilon \to |(x - 4)| < \dfrac{\varepsilon}{|x+4|}$

So, $|x - 4| < \sigma \simeq \dfrac{\varepsilon}{|x+4|}$

Infinite Limits: $\qquad \lim\limits_{x \to \infty} \dfrac{1}{x} \to 0$

Divide all inner terms by the leading term in the denominator and plug in infinity.

Ex. 2: $\lim\limits_{x \to \infty} \dfrac{2x^2 + 3x + 4}{5x^2 + 7x + 9} \to \lim\limits_{x \to \infty} \dfrac{\frac{2x^2}{x^2} + \frac{3x}{x^2} + \frac{4}{x^2}}{\frac{5x^2}{x^2} + \frac{7x}{x^2} + \frac{9}{x^2}} \to \lim\limits_{x \to \infty} \dfrac{2 + \frac{3}{x} + \frac{4}{x^2}}{5 + \frac{7}{x} + \frac{9}{x^2}} \to \dfrac{2 + \frac{3}{\infty} + \frac{4}{\infty}}{5 + \frac{7}{\infty} + \frac{9}{\infty}} \to \dfrac{2 + 0 + 0}{5 + 0 + 0} \to \left\{\dfrac{2}{5}\right\}$

Limit Theorems

$\lim\limits_{x \to 0} \dfrac{\sin x}{x} = 1$ $\qquad\qquad\qquad \lim\limits_{x \to 0} \dfrac{1 - \cos x}{x} = 0$

Horizontal and Vertical Asymptotes using Limits

$\lim\limits_{x \to \pm\infty} f(x) = c \to$ HA: $y = c$ $\qquad \lim\limits_{x \to c\pm} f(x) = \pm\infty \to$ VA: $x = c$

Squeeze Theorem

$-1 \le \sin x \le 1$ $\qquad\qquad\qquad\qquad -1 \le \cos x \le 1$

$-\dfrac{1}{x} \le \dfrac{\sin x}{x} \le \dfrac{1}{x}$ $\qquad\qquad\qquad -\dfrac{1}{x} \le \dfrac{\cos x}{x} \le \dfrac{1}{x}$

$\lim\limits_{x \to \infty} -\dfrac{1}{x} \le \lim\limits_{x \to \infty} \dfrac{\sin x}{x} \le \lim\limits_{x \to \infty} \dfrac{1}{x}$ $\qquad \lim\limits_{x \to \infty} -\dfrac{1}{x} \le \lim\limits_{x \to \infty} \dfrac{\cos x}{x} \le \lim\limits_{x \to \infty} \dfrac{1}{x}$

$0 \le \lim\limits_{x \to \infty} \dfrac{\sin x}{x} \le 0$ $\qquad\qquad\qquad 0 \le \lim\limits_{x \to \infty} \dfrac{\cos x}{x} \le 0$

$\lim\limits_{x \to \infty} \dfrac{\sin x}{x} = 0$ $\qquad\qquad\qquad\qquad \lim\limits_{x \to \infty} \dfrac{\cos x}{x} = 0$

This is useful when taking the infinite limits of trigonometric functions.

Differentiation

Derivative Definition

Consider the derivative as the rate of change of any function. The slope one worked with in previous chapters was the rate of change of linear functions.

Limit Method

$$f'(x) = \lim_{\Delta x \to 0} \frac{f(x+\Delta x)-f(x)}{\Delta x}$$

Notice the equation resembles difference quotient. (Refer to page 69)

Ex. 1: Find the derivative. $\quad f(x) = \frac{x-1}{x+2}$

$$f(x+h) = \frac{(x+h)-1}{(x+h)+2} \rightarrow f(x+h) = \frac{x+h-1}{x+h+2}$$

$$\lim_{\Delta x \to 0} \frac{f(x+\Delta x)-f(x)}{\Delta x} \rightarrow \lim_{h \to 0} \frac{\frac{x+h-1}{x+h+2} - \frac{x-1}{x+2}}{h} \rightarrow \lim_{h \to 0} \frac{\frac{(x+h-1)(x+2)-(x-1)(x+h+2)}{(x+h+2)(x+2)}}{h} \rightarrow$$

$$\lim_{h \to 0} \frac{(x+h-1)(x+2)-(x-1)(x+h+2)}{h(x+h+2)(x+2)} \rightarrow \lim_{h \to 0} \frac{x^2+x+xh+2h-2-x^2-x-xh+h+2}{h(x+h+2)(x+2)} \rightarrow$$

$$\lim_{h \to 0} \frac{3h}{h(x+h+2)(x+2)} \rightarrow \lim_{h \to 0} \frac{3}{(x+h+2)(x+2)} \rightarrow \frac{3}{(x+(0)+2)(x+2)} \rightarrow \left\{ \frac{3}{(x+2)^2} \right\}$$

Primary Identities

Power Rule: $\qquad \frac{d}{dx}[x^n] = nx^{n-1}$

Product Rule: $\qquad \frac{d}{dx}[uv] = u'v + uv'$

Quotient Rule: $\qquad \frac{d}{dx}\left[\frac{u}{v}\right] = \frac{u'v-uv'}{v^2}$

Chain Rule: $\qquad \frac{d}{dx}[f(u)] = f'(u) \cdot u'$

Differentiation

Ex. 2: Find the derivative. $\quad f(x) = (x^2 - 4)(x + 3)$

$$u = x^2 - 4 \rightarrow u' = 2x \qquad\qquad v = x + 3 \rightarrow v' = 1$$

$$u'v + uv' \rightarrow (2x)(x + 3) + (x^2 - 4)(1) \rightarrow \{3x^2 + 6x - 4\}$$

Ex. 3: Find the derivative. $\quad f(x) = \frac{x-1}{x+2}$

$$u = x - 1 \rightarrow u' = 1 \qquad\qquad v = x + 2 \rightarrow v' = 1$$

$$\frac{u'v - uv'}{v^2} \rightarrow \frac{(1)(x+2) - (x-1)(1)}{(x+2)^2} \rightarrow \frac{x+2-x+1}{(x+2)^2} \rightarrow \left\{\frac{3}{(x+2)^2}\right\}$$

Ex. 4: Find the derivative. $\quad f(x) = (4x^3 + 2x^2 - 3)^4$

$$u = 4x^3 + 2x^2 - 3 \rightarrow u' = 12x^2 + 4x$$

$$f(u) = u^4 \rightarrow f'(u) = 4u^3 \cdot u' \rightarrow \{4(4x^3 + 2x^2 - 3)^3 \cdot (12x^2 + 4x)\}$$

Initial Trigonometric Identities

$$\frac{d}{dx}[\sin x] = \cos x \qquad \frac{d}{dx}[\tan x] = \sec^2 x \qquad \frac{d}{dx}[\sec x] = \sec x \tan x$$

$$\frac{d}{dx}[\cos x] = -\sin x \qquad \frac{d}{dx}[\cot x] = -\csc^2 x \qquad \frac{d}{dx}[\csc x] = -\csc x \cot x$$

Implicit Differentiation and Related Rates

Normally, one would take the derivative in respect to x ($\frac{d}{dx}$), but when one differentiates expressions with variables not matching the respect variable, one must leave a derivative notation to compensate for the difference ($\frac{dy}{dx}$ for example). Related Rates uses this method in applications commonly with respect to time (Example: $\frac{dV}{dt}$ which is change in Volume with respect to time).

Differentiation

Ex. 5: Given a conical tank containing liquid ethanol fills at a rate of 12.0 cubic feet per minute with its point aimed downward and its height being 25.0 feet and radius of 12.5 feet. Find the instantaneous rates of depth and surface area of the liquid inside the cone given at a current depth of 10.0 feet and radius of the surface of the liquid as 5.0 feet.

$$\frac{r}{h} = \frac{12.5}{25.0} \rightarrow \frac{r}{h} = \frac{1}{2} \rightarrow h = 2r \rightarrow r = \frac{1}{2}h$$

$$V = \frac{\pi}{3}r^2 h \rightarrow V = \frac{\pi}{3}\left(\frac{1}{2}h\right)^2 h \rightarrow V = \frac{\pi}{12}h^3 \rightarrow \frac{dV}{dt} = \frac{\pi}{4}h^2 \cdot \frac{dh}{dt}$$

$$\frac{dV}{dt} = \frac{\pi}{4}h^2 \cdot \frac{dh}{dt} \rightarrow (12.0) = \frac{\pi}{4}(10.0)^2 \cdot \frac{dh}{dt} \rightarrow 12 = 25\pi \cdot \frac{dh}{dt} \rightarrow \frac{dh}{dt} = \frac{12}{25\pi}$$

$$r = \frac{1}{2}h \rightarrow \frac{dr}{dt} = \frac{1}{2} \cdot \frac{dh}{dt} \rightarrow \frac{dr}{dt} = \frac{1}{2} \cdot \frac{12}{25\pi} \rightarrow \frac{dr}{dt} = \frac{6}{25\pi}$$

$$SA = \pi r^2 \rightarrow \frac{dSA}{dt} = 2\pi r \cdot \frac{dr}{dt} \rightarrow \frac{dSA}{dt} = 2\pi(5.0) \cdot \frac{6}{25\pi} \rightarrow \frac{dSA}{dt} = \frac{12}{5}$$

Solution: **The rate of depth is increasing by $\frac{12}{25\pi}$ feet per minute and the rate of surface area is increasing by $\frac{12}{5}$ square feet per minute.**

Position, Velocity, and Acceleration Relation

Position: $p(x)$

Velocity: $v(x) = p'(x)$ First Derivative

Acceleration: $a(x) = v'(x) = p''(x)$ Second Derivative

Differentiation

Extrema and First Derivative Test

1. Take the derivative of the function.
2. Set the derivative equal to zero.
3. Test values between those zeros to figure out if the function is increasing or decreasing. $f'(x) = (+)$ or $f'(x) = (-)$
4. Maximum: Increasing to decreasing
   Minimum: Decreasing to increasing

Concavity and the Second Derivative Test

1. Take the second derivative of the function.
2. Set the second derivative equal to zero.
3. Test values between those zeros to figure out if the function is concaving up or concaving down. $f''(x) = (+)$ or $f''(x) = (-)$

Point of Inflection: the concavity changes and is differentiable.

Newton's Method

1. Guess the first approximation.
2. Find sequential approximations using this equation: $x_{n+1} = x_n - \dfrac{f(x_n)}{f'(x_n)}$

Differentiation

Ex. 6: Approximate $\sqrt[5]{7}$ using Newton's Method by three decimal places.

$$x = \sqrt[5]{7} \rightarrow x^5 = 7 \rightarrow x^5 - 7 = 0 \rightarrow f(x) = x^5 - 7 \rightarrow f'(x) = 5x^4$$

Set up a table:

$$f(x) = x^5 - 7 \qquad\qquad f'(x) = 5x^4$$

n	x_n	$f(x_n)$	$f'(x_n)$	$\dfrac{f(x_n)}{f'(x_n)}$	$x_n - \dfrac{f(x_n)}{f'(x_n)}$
1	1.000	−6.000	5.000	−1.200	2.200
2	2.200	44.536	117.128	0.380	1.820
3	1.820	12.956	54.831	0.236	1.583
4	1.583	2.955	31.435	0.094	1.489
5	1.489	0.331	24.609	0.013	1.476
6	1.476	0.006	23.732	0.00025	1.476

Solution: **The approximation of $\sqrt[5]{7}$ is 1.476.**

Integration

Integration Definition

The polar opposite to the derivative, the integral (anti-derivative) can be used to find the area under a curve.

Common Integrals (Identities)

$$\int kx^n \, dx = \frac{k}{n+1} x^{n+1} + C \qquad k\text{: Coefficient (constant)}$$

$$\int \frac{1}{x} dx = \ln|x| + C \qquad\qquad \int k^x \, dx = \frac{k^x}{\ln k} + C$$

$$\int \sin x \, dx = -\cos x + C \qquad\qquad \int \cos x \, dx = \sin x + C$$

$$\int \tan x \, dx = -\ln|\cos x| + C \qquad\qquad \int \cot x \, dx = \ln|\sin x| + C$$

Others are listed in Appendix E.

Substitution Rule

Let u equal the more complex part of the exercise, find the derivative of u, and then substitute in u and the derivative of u (du) into the integral.

Ex. 1: Find the integral. $\int x^2 (x^3 + 27)^{\frac{4}{3}} \, dx$

$$u = x^3 + 27 \rightarrow du = 3x^2 \, dx$$

$$\frac{1}{3}\int (x^3 + 27)^{\frac{4}{3}}(3x^2) \, dx \rightarrow \frac{1}{3}\int u^{\frac{4}{3}} \, du \rightarrow \frac{1}{3} \cdot \frac{3}{7} u^{\frac{7}{3}} + C \rightarrow \left\{ \frac{1}{7}(x^3 + 27)^{\frac{7}{3}} + C \right\}$$

In more detail: First, let u equal the more complex portion of the equation. Second, take the derivative of the u equation to get du. Third, compensate for the du substitution by attaching the needed coefficient and its reciprocal. Fourth, substitute u and du into the integral. Fifth, integrate normally and add C when necessary. Finally, replace u with the expression in terms of x.

Integration

Helpful way to remember to add C: "Don't forget your cookie!"

<u>Integration by parts</u>

$$\int u \, dv = uv - \int v \, du$$

Ex. 2: $\int (x^3 + 14)e^x \, dx$

$u = x^3 + 14 \to du = 3x^2 \, dx \qquad\qquad dv = e^x \, dx \to v = e^x$

$uv - \int v \, du \to (x^3 + 14)(e^x) - \int e^x(3x^2) \, dx$

$u = 3x^2 \to du = 6x \, dx \qquad\qquad dv = e^x \, dx \to v = e^x$

$(x^3 + 14)(e^x) - [(3x^2)(e^x) - \int e^x(6x)dx]$
$(x^3 - 3x^2 + 14)(e^x) + \int e^x(6x)dx$

$u = 6x \to du = 6 \, dx \qquad\qquad dv = e^x \, dx \to v = e^x$

$(x^3 - 3x^2 + 14)(e^x) + (6x)(e^x) - \int e^x(6)dx$
$(x^3 - 3x^2 + 14)(e^x) + (6x)(e^x) - 6e^x + C$
$\{(x^3 - 3x^2 + 6x + 8)(e^x) + C\}$

<u>Trigonometric Substitution</u>

Expression	Substitution	Final Expression
$\sqrt{a^2 - u^2}$	$u = a \sin\theta$ $du = a \cos\theta \, d\theta$	$\sqrt{a^2 - u^2} \to a \cos\theta$ $"1 - \sin^2\theta = \cos^2\theta"$
$\sqrt{u^2 - a^2}$	$u = a \sec\theta$ $du = a \sec\theta \tan\theta \, d\theta$	$\sqrt{u^2 - a^2} \to a \tan\theta$ $"\sec^2\theta - 1 = \tan^2\theta"$
$\sqrt{u^2 + a^2}$	$u = a \tan\theta$ $du = a \sec^2\theta \, d\theta$	$\sqrt{u^2 + a^2} \to a \sec\theta$ $"\tan^2\theta + 1 = \sec^2\theta"$

Integration

If the expression cannot be obtained directly, then complete the square to obtain the desired expression. Also, a right triangle is useful for substituting between x and θ.

Ex. 3: $\int \dfrac{\sqrt{9-4x^2}}{16x^2}\,dx$ $\qquad\qquad \sqrt{a^2-u^2} \rightarrow u = a\sin\theta$

$$2x = 3\sin\theta \rightarrow x = \frac{3}{2}\sin\theta \rightarrow dx = \frac{3}{2}\cos\theta\,d\theta$$

$$\int \frac{\sqrt{9-4\left(\frac{3}{2}\sin\theta\right)^2}}{16\left(\frac{3}{2}\sin\theta\right)^2}\cdot\frac{3}{2}\cos\theta\,d\theta$$

$$\int \frac{\sqrt{9-9\sin^2\theta}}{36\sin^2\theta}\cdot\frac{3}{2}\cos\theta\,d\theta$$

$$\int \frac{\sqrt{9\cos^2\theta}}{24\sin^2\theta}\cdot\cos\theta\,d\theta$$

$$\int \frac{3\cos\theta}{24\sin^2\theta}\cdot\cos\theta\,d\theta$$

$$\frac{1}{8}\int \frac{\cos^2\theta}{\sin^2\theta}\,d\theta$$

$$\frac{1}{8}\int \cot^2\theta\,d\theta$$

$$\frac{1}{8}\int (\csc^2\theta - 1)\,d\theta$$

$$\frac{1}{8}(-\cot\theta - \theta) + C$$

$$\frac{1}{8}\left(-\frac{\sqrt{9-4x^2}}{2x} - \sin^{-1}\left(\frac{2x}{3}\right)\right) + C$$

$$\left\{-\frac{\sqrt{9-4x^2}}{16x} - \frac{1}{8}\sin^{-1}\left(\frac{2x}{3}\right) + C\right\}$$

Integration

Partial Fractions

Ex. 4: $\int \frac{9x^2+16x-24}{x^3+3x^2-10x-24}\,dx$

Factor the denominator: $x^3 + 3x^2 - 10x - 24$

```
-2| 1   3  -10  -24        x² + x - 12
        -2   -2   24
   _____     (x - 3)(x + 4)
    1   1  -12 | 0
```
(x+2)

Factored Form: $(x + 2)(x - 3)(x + 4)$

$\int \frac{9x^2+16x-24}{(x+2)(x-3)(x+4)}\,dx$

$\frac{9x^2+16x-24}{(x+2)(x-3)(x+4)} = \frac{A}{x+2} + \frac{B}{x-3} + \frac{C}{x+4}$

$9x^2 + 16x - 24 = A(x - 3)(x + 4) + B(x + 2)(x + 4) + C(x + 2)(x - 3)$

Let $x = -2$:

$9(-2)^2 + 16(-2) - 24 = A(-2 - 3)(-2 + 4) \rightarrow -10A = -20 \rightarrow A = 2$

Let $x = 3$:

$9(3)^2 + 16(3) - 24 = B(3 + 2)(3 + 4) \rightarrow 35B = 105 \rightarrow B = 3$

Let $x = -4$:

$9(-4)^2 + 16(-4) - 24 = C(-4 + 2)(-4 - 3) \rightarrow 14C = 56 \rightarrow C = 4$

$\int \frac{2}{x+2} + \frac{3}{x-3} + \frac{4}{x+4}\,dx$

$\{2\ln|x + 2| + 3\ln|x - 3| + 4\ln|x + 4| + C\}$

Integration

Geometric Integrals

Volume Disk $\quad \pi \int_a^b \left(f(x)\right)^2 dx$

Volume Washer $\quad \pi \int_a^b \left(f(x)\right)^2 - \left(g(x)\right)^2 dx$

Volume Shell $\quad 2\pi \int_a^b x f(x)\, dx$

Arc Length $\quad L = \int_a^b \sqrt{1 + (y')^2}\, dx$

Surface Area $\quad SA = 2\pi \int_a^b f(x)\sqrt{1 + \left(f'(x)\right)^2}\, dx$

Author's Note: I only provided a few examples in this chapter only to show the main concepts within Integration. I did not provide examples for the Geometric Integrals as the concept is deep into Calculus. Once a student has reached Calculus, the student should have a strong knowledge of Mathematics and should be able to construct further techniques on his or her own. I chose this point to stop the Math section of this journal. I wish not to include concepts beyond Calculus as I have yet to master levels of Math beyond Calculus. To those of who reach such a level of Math, I commend you. Reaching such a level of Math requires incredible skill and insight to march forth.

Conversion Factors

<u>Metric System</u>

	kilo-	hecto-	deka-	BASE	deci-	centi-	milli-			micro-			nano-			pico-
	k	h	da	BASE	d	c	m			mc			n			p

Method 1: Shift the decimal (Base unit will be meters for this set of examples)

Ex. 1: Convert 0.14 km (kilometer) to mm (millimeter).

Shift 6   0.140000,   **140, 000 mm**

Method 2: Base ten direct conversion

Ex. 2: Convert 0.027 km (kilometer) to μm (micrometer). (Note: μ = mc)

9 decimal places between km to μm → 1 km = 1,000,000,000 μm

$(0.027 \text{ km}) \left(\frac{1,000,000,000 \text{ μm}}{1 \text{ km}} \right) →$ **27, 000, 000 μm**

One must understand that the metric system is a base ten system. The methods above are useful for direct metric conversion, but Chemistry uses the second method structure more often as conversions within Chemistry tend to use two or more conversion factors in each calculation. Also, the following conversion factors can be used in conjunction to method 2:

1 km = 1000 m

1 m   = 1000 mm   1 m = 100 cm (centimeter)

1 mm = 1000 μm

1 μm = 1000 nm

1 nm = 1000 pm

Conversion Factors

Dimensional Analysis (Memorization Required)

1 mile (mi)	=	5280 feet
1 mile	=	1760 yards
1 mile	=	1.6093 km
1 inch	=	2.54 cm
1 Å	=	10^{-10} m
1 pound (lb) =		16 oz
1 lb	=	453.59 grams (g)
1 oz	=	28.3 grams (g)
1 kg	=	2.2046 lb
1 calorie	=	4.184 Joules (J) [J = kg m^2 / s^2]
1 Liter (L)	=	1.0567 quarts
1 gallon	=	4 quarts
1 gallon	=	3.7854 L
1 mL	=	1 cm^3
1 atm	=	760 mmHg
1 atm	=	760 torr
1 atm	=	101.325 kPa
1 atm	=	14.70 lb / in^2

Ex. 3: Convert 240. lb to kg

$$(240.\,\text{lb}) \left(\frac{1\ \text{kg}}{2.2046\ \text{lb}} \right) \rightarrow \textbf{109 kg}$$

Ex. 4: Convert 450. mi to km

$$(450.\,\text{mi}) \left(\frac{1.6093\ \text{km}}{1\ \text{mi}} \right) \rightarrow \textbf{724 km}$$

Conversion Factors

<u>Temperature</u>

Convert Fahrenheit to Celsius: $C = \frac{5}{9}(F - 32)$

Convert Celsius to Fahrenheit: $F = \frac{9}{5}C + 32$

Convert Celsius to Kelvin: $K = C + 273.15$

Ex. 5: The normal temperature of the human body is 98.6 Fahrenheit. Convert this temperature to Celsius and Kelvin.

$$C = \frac{5}{9}(98.6 - 32) \rightarrow C = \frac{5}{9}(66.6) \rightarrow C = 37.0 \rightarrow \textbf{37.0° C}$$

$$K = 37.0 + 273.15 \rightarrow K = 310.15 \rightarrow \textbf{310.2 K}$$

Author's Note: To make sure you have the temperature equations correct, just remember the two normal human body temperatures of 98.6° F and 37.0° C. Both are worth knowing inside and outside of Chemistry.

You may have noticed that I rounded my previous answers while there was no instruction to do so. In Chemistry (along with Physics and other sciences), use a methodology of rounding called "Significant Figures."

Significant Figures

Given a number, going left to right, start counting significant figures once one reads the first non-zero digit. Keep counting until the number ends OR once the number only has zeros remaining and there is no decimal point within the number.

Exact values represent infinitely many significant figures. For example, within the formula $V = \frac{4}{3}\pi r^3$, $\frac{4}{3}$ is treated as an exact value. The conversion factor for inches to centimeters (1 inch = 2.54 cm) is also treated as an exact value.

<u>Count the significant figures (SF)</u>

Ex. 1: 34.567 → **5 SF**   Ex. 2: 0.00418 → **3SF**

Ex. 3: 1400 → **2 SF**   Ex. 4: 3.4001×10^4 → **5 SF**

<u>Rules within Calculations</u>

1. When multiplying and/or dividing values, the result will keep the lowest SF among the values.
2. When adding and/or subtracting values, keep the lowest number of decimal places among the values.

Ex. 5: (14.86)(1.39)(24.61) → <u>508</u>.329394 → **508**

Ex. 6: 36.17 + 8.631 + 12.194 → <u>56.99</u>5 → **57.00**

Ex. 7: (1.23+4.2)(18.6-3.42) → (<u>5.43</u>)(<u>15.18</u>) → <u>82</u>.4274 → **82**

Ex. 8: (7.53+5.27)(4.87-3.96) → (<u>12.80</u>)(0.<u>91</u>) → <u>11</u>.648 → **12**

Nomenclature Basics of Chemistry

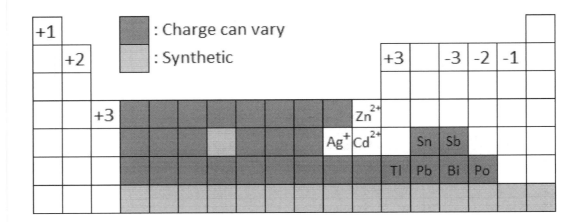

The Periodic Table above also contains common charges of select groups.

Metal with a Nonmetal

Cation: keep the same name. Use Roman Numerals to denote the charge of elements that vary in charge (Most Transition Metals, Sn, Sb, Tl, Pb, Bi, and Po).

Anion: replace the last part with –ide, –ate, or –ite.
    Single Element: use –ide at the end.
    Bonded with Oxygen (Oxyanions): use –ate or –ite at the end.

Other Polyatomic Ions: $C_2H_3O_2^-$ (acetate), OH^- (hydroxide), NH_4^+ (ammonium), CN^- (cyanide), N_3^- (azide), SCN^- (thiocyanate), $C_2O_4^{2-}$ (oxalate), etc.

Nonmetal with a Nonmetal

First element: keep the same name, and then add a prefix based on its subscript if its subscript is above one.
Second element: replace the end with –ide, and then add a prefix based on its subscript. (Note: oxides of this set tend to remove the last 'a' of select prefixes.)

Prefix: (1) mono-   (2) di-   (3) tri-   (4) tetra-   (5) penta-
               (6) hexa-   (7) hepto-   (8) octa-   (9) nona-   (10) deca-

Nomenclature Basics of Chemistry

Oxyanions

Periodic Table	C N Cl Br I		P S As Se Te	
	N	Cl, Br, I	S, Se, Te	P, As
Charge	-1	-1	-2	-3
Per- -ate		ClO_4^-		
-ate	NO_3^-	ClO_3^-	SO_4^{2-}	PO_4^{3-}
-ite	NO_2^-	ClO_2^-	SO_3^{2-}	PO_3^{3-}
Hypo- -ite		ClO^-	SO_2^{2-}	PO_2^{3-}

Carbonate: CO_3^{2-} Permanganate: MnO_4^-

Chromate: CrO_4^{2-} Dichromate: $Cr_2O_7^{2-}$

Acid Naming

Anion Name	Acid Name	Example	
–ide	Hydro- -ic Acid	HCl	(Hydrochloric Acid)
–ate	-ic Acid	HNO_3	(Nitric Acid)
–ite	-ous Acid	H_3PO_3	(Phosphorous Acid)

Stoichiometry

Balancing Equations

1. Focus on the most complex compound and balance its elements first. (One can also balance via ions if the ions remain intact.)
2. Check for matching elements (ions) between the two sides.
3. To balance, use the LCD between the elements (ions) currently involved.
4. Continue to balance in a chain between the two sides using the previous steps. Leave the singular elementals for last as one can force balance those with fractions. To eliminate fractions, multiply the equation by the LCD of all fractions within the problem.

Ex. 1: Balance: $\underline{C_4H_{10}}\text{ (g)} + O_2\text{ (g)} \rightarrow CO_2\text{ (g)} + H_2O\text{ (g)}$

$C_4H_{10}\text{ (g)} + \underline{O_2\text{ (g)}} \rightarrow 4\ CO_2\text{ (g)} + 5\ H_2O\text{ (g)}$

$C_4H_{10}\text{ (g)} + \dfrac{13}{2}\ O_2\text{ (g)} \rightarrow 4\ CO_2\text{ (g)} + 5\ H_2O\text{ (g)}$

$[2][\ C_4H_{10}\text{ (g)} + \dfrac{13}{2}\ O_2\text{ (g)} \rightarrow 4\ CO_2\text{ (g)} + 5\ H_2O\text{ (g)}\ ]$

$2\ C_4H_{10}\text{ (g)} + 13\ O_2\text{ (g)} \rightarrow 8\ CO_2\text{ (g)} + 10\ H_2O\text{ (g)}$

Ex. 2: Balance: $H_3PO_4\text{ (aq)} + Ca(OH)_2\text{ (aq)} \rightarrow \underline{Ca_3(PO_4)_2}\text{ (s)} + H_2O\text{ (l)}$

$H_3PO_4\text{ (aq)} + \underline{3Ca(OH)_2}\text{ (aq)} \rightarrow Ca_3(PO_4)_2\text{ (s)} + H_2O\text{ (l)}$

$H_3PO_4\text{ (aq)} + 3Ca(OH)_2\text{ (aq)} \rightarrow Ca_3(PO_4)_2\text{ (s)} + \underline{6H_2O}\text{ (l)}$

$2H_3PO_4\text{ (aq)} + 3Ca(OH)_2\text{ (aq)} \rightarrow Ca_3(PO_4)_2\text{ (s)} + 6H_2O\text{ (l)}$

Determine Empirical / Molecular Formulas

1. Convert all elemental masses to moles.
2. Divide all mole values by the lowest among them.
3. If needed, multiply all mole ratios by an integer to convert the decimal values to integers. (This will give the Empirical Formula)
4. Divide Molar Mass by Empirical Mass to obtain their ratio and convert the Empirical Formula to Molecular Formula.

Stoichiometry

Ex. 3: Given 360.0 grams of Carbon, 60.43 grams of Hydrogen, and 480.0 grams of Oxygen find the Empirical Formula and Molecular Formula if the Molar Mass is 180.156 grams per mole.

$\dfrac{360.0 \text{ g C}}{12.01 \text{ g/mol}}$ → 29.98 mol C → $\dfrac{29.98 \text{ mol C}}{29.98 \text{ mol}}$ → 1 C   Empirical: **CH₂O**

$\dfrac{60.43 \text{ g H}}{1.008 \text{ g/mol}}$ → 59.95 mol H → $\dfrac{59.95 \text{ mol H}}{29.98 \text{ mol}}$ → 2 H   12.01 + 2(1.008) + 16.00

$\dfrac{480.0 \text{ g O}}{16.00 \text{ g/mol}}$ → 30.00 mol O → $\dfrac{30.00 \text{ mol O}}{29.98 \text{ mol}}$ → 1 O   Empirical Mass: 30.026

$\dfrac{180.156}{30.026}$ → 6   [6][CH₂O] → C₆H₁₂O₆   Molecular: **C₆H₁₂O₆**

Limiting Reactant and Percent Yield

1. Convert both initial values to a single target compound or molecule.
2. The Limiting Reactant gives the lesser of the two. This also declares the Theoretical Yield.
3. Given an Actual Yield, use this equation to find the Percent Yield:

$$\dfrac{[\text{Actual Yield}]}{[\text{Theoretical Yield}]} \times 100\% = [\text{Percent Yield}]$$

Ex. 4:   3 Pb(NO₃)₂ (aq) + 2 Na₃PO₄ (aq) → Pb₃(PO₄)₂ (s) + 6 NaNO₃ (aq)
Given 50.0 grams of Pb(NO₃)₂ [331.22 g/mol] and 50.0 grams of Na₃PO₄ [163.94 g/mol], what's the limiting reactant, theoretical yield, and percent yield given 34.4 grams of Pb₃(PO₄)₂ [811.54 g/mol] was obtained?

$$(50.0 \text{ g Pb(NO}_3)_2) \left(\dfrac{\text{mol Pb(NO}_3)_2}{331.22 \text{ g Pb(NO}_3)_2} \right) \left(\dfrac{\text{mol Pb}_3(\text{PO}_4)_2}{3 \text{ mol Pb(NO}_3)_2} \right) \left(\dfrac{811.54 \text{ g Pb}_3(\text{PO}_4)_2}{\text{mol Pb}_3(\text{PO}_4)_2} \right) \rightarrow$$

<u>40.8</u>359 g Pb₃(PO₄)₂ Theoretical Yield: **40.8 g Pb₃(PO₄)₂** Limiting: **Pb(NO₃)₂**

$$(50.0 \text{ g Na}_3\text{PO}_4) \left(\dfrac{\text{mol Na}_3\text{PO}_4}{163.94 \text{ g Na}_3\text{PO}_4} \right) \left(\dfrac{\text{mol Pb}_3(\text{PO}_4)_2}{2 \text{ mol Na}_3\text{PO}_4} \right) \left(\dfrac{811.54 \text{ g Pb}_3(\text{PO}_4)_2}{\text{mol Pb}_3(\text{PO}_4)_2} \right) \rightarrow$$

<u>123</u>.756 g Pb₃(PO₄)₂

$\dfrac{34.4 \text{ g}}{40.8359 \text{ g}}$ x 100% → <u>84.2</u>396% Percent Yield: **84.2%**

States of Matter and Basic Reactions

States of Matter (Single Element and Diatomic)

Gas (g): H, N, O, F, Cl, and Noble gases (Standard Lab Conditions)
Liquid (l): Br and Hg (Standard Lab Conditions)
Solid (s): All other elements (Standard Lab Conditions)
Aqueous (aq): Compounds in solution which are soluble

Solubility Rules (For a more detailed list, go to page 178: Electrolytes)
Always Soluble: Alkali Metals, NH_4^+, NO_3^-, $C_2H_3O_2^-$, ClO_3^-, and ClO_4^-.

Generally Soluble:	Cl^-, Br^-, and I^- (except with Ag, Hg, Pb)
	SO_4^{2-} (except with Hg, Pb, Sr, Ba)
Generally Insoluble:	OH^- (except with Ca, Sr, Ba)
	CO_3^{2-}, PO_4^{3-}, CrO_4^{2-}, S^{2-}, F^-

Note: Solubility Rules can vary depending on the textbook used.

Basic Reactions

Single Displacement:	$A + BC \rightarrow AC + B$
Double Displacement:	$AB + CD \rightarrow AD + CB$
Combination:	$A + B \rightarrow AB$
Decomposition:	$AB \rightarrow A + B$
Combustion (Reacts w/ O_2):	$C_xH_y + O_2 \rightarrow CO_2 + H_2O$
	$C_xH_yO_z + O_2 \rightarrow CO_2 + H_2O$

Diatomic List

$H_2(g)$ $N_2(g)$ $O_2(g)$ $F_2(g)$ $Cl_2(g)$ $Br_2(l)$ $I_2(s)$

Aqueous Solutions

Net Ionic Equations

1. Within the Molecular equation, break down all substances that are strong electrolytes and aqueous into ions. (Electrolytes: Page 178)
2. Cancel out matching ions on both sides.
3. The result is the Net Ionic Equation.

Acid-Base Neutralization

Acid (H^+) + Base (OH^-) → Salt + Water

Ex. 1: Hunter and Gauge wish to do a Chemical experiment involving a mini volcano. Besides the red food coloring, the actual reaction requires Baking Soda ($NaHCO_3$) and Vinegar ($HC_2H_3O_2$). Find the Net Ionic Equation.

$NaHCO_3$ (aq) + $HC_2H_3O_2$ (aq) → $NaC_2H_3O_2$ (aq) + H_2CO_3 (aq)

H_2CO_3 (aq) → H_2O (l) + CO_2 (g) (Carbonic Acid readily decomposes.)

$NaHCO_3$ (aq) + $HC_2H_3O_2$ (aq) → $NaC_2H_3O_2$ (aq) + H_2O (l) + CO_2 (g) [Molecular]

Na^+ + HCO_3^- + $HC_2H_3O_2$ → Na^+ + $C_2H_3O_2^-$ + H_2O (l) + CO_2 (g) [Total Ionic]

HCO_3^- (aq) + $HC_2H_3O_2$ (aq) → $C_2H_3O_2^-$(aq) + H_2O (l) + CO_2 (g) [Net Ionic Equation]

Oxidation-Reduction (Redox)

Definition: transfer of electrons between elements.

Ex. 2: Declare which elements are oxidized or reduced.

Zn (s) + 2 $AgNO_3$ (aq) → $Zn(NO_3)_2$ (aq) + 2 Ag (s)

Zn (s) + 2 Ag^+ (aq) + 2 NO_3^- (aq) → Zn^{2+} (aq) + 2 NO_3^- (aq) + 2 Ag (s)

Zn^0 (s) → Zn^{2+} (aq) [More Positive: Lost Electrons: Oxidized]

Ag^+ (aq) → Ag^0 (s) [More Negative: Gained Elections: Reduced]

Oxidized: Zn   Reduced: Ag

Aqueous Solutions

In example 2 on page 157, if the solid metal is higher in the Activity Series, then it'll take the other metal's partner (anion). The following table provides the ranking system of many elements in regards to ease of oxidation (Activity Series):

1. $Li \rightarrow Li^+ + e^-$	7. $Al \rightarrow Al^{3+} + 3e^-$	13. $Co \rightarrow Co^{2+} + 2e^-$	19. $Ag \rightarrow Ag^+ + e^-$
2. $K \rightarrow K^+ + e^-$	8. $Mn \rightarrow Mn^{2+} + 2e^-$	14. $Ni \rightarrow Ni^{2+} + 2e^-$	20. $Hg \rightarrow Hg^{2+} + 2e^-$
3. $Ba \rightarrow Ba^{2+} + 2e^-$	9. $Zn \rightarrow Zn^{2+} + 2e^-$	15. $Sn \rightarrow Sn^{2+} + 2e^-$	21. $Pt \rightarrow Pt^{2+} + 2e^-$
4. $Ca \rightarrow Ca^{2+} + 2e^-$	10. $Cr \rightarrow Cr^{3+} + 3e^-$	16. $Pb \rightarrow Pb^{2+} + 2e^-$	22. $Au \rightarrow Au^{3+} + 3e^-$
5. $Na \rightarrow Na^+ + e^-$	11. $Fe \rightarrow Fe^{2+} + 2e^-$	17. $H_2 \rightarrow 2H^+ + 2e^-$	
6. $Mg \rightarrow Mg^{2+} + 2e^-$	12. $Cd \rightarrow Cd^{2+} + 2e^-$	18. $Cu \rightarrow Cu^{2+} + 2e^-$	

Oxidation Numbers

Elemental State (Single Element and Diatomic) = 0

Alkali Metal Ions = +1   Alkaline Earth Metal Ions = +2

Boron Group Ions = +3   Sc and Y Ions = +3

Hydrogen = +1 (bonded with nonmetals) or -1 (bonded with metals)

Oxygen = -2 (in most situations) or -1 (as Peroxide ion)

Halogens = -1 (when bonded with metals, carbon, and hydrogen)

Precipitation Reaction (Two aqueous solutions mix to yield a solid)

Ex. 3: What is the precipitate formed when aqueous sodium chloride and aqueous lead (ii) nitrate combine?

$NaCl$ (aq) + $Pb(NO_3)_2$ (aq) → ?

$NaCl$ (aq) + $Pb(NO_3)_2$ (aq) → $NaNO_3$ (?) + $PbCl_2$ (?) [Solubility / Balance]

2 $NaCl$ (aq) + $Pb(NO_3)_2$ (aq) → 2 $NaNO_3$ (aq) + $PbCl_2$ (s)

Precipitate Formed: $PbCl_2$

Aqueous Solutions

Calculations of Dilution and Neutralization Reactions

$$M_1V_1 = M_2V_2 \quad \text{OR} \quad M_1V_1 + M_2V_2 = M_3V_3$$

Ex. 4: How many mL of 5.00 M HCl are needed to obtain 40.0 mL of 0.100 M HCl?

$M_1 = 5.00$ M $\qquad M_2 = 0.100$ M $\qquad V_2 = 40.0$ mL

$M_1V_1 = M_2V_2 \rightarrow V_1 = \frac{M_2V_2}{M_1} \rightarrow V_1 = \frac{(0.100 \text{ M})(40.0 \text{ mL})}{(5.00 \text{ M})} \rightarrow V_1 = \mathbf{0.800 \ mL}$

Neutralization Reactions can also use the $M_1V_1 = M_2V_2$ equation as long as the reactants are one-to-one (number of moles) within the chemical equation.

Ex. 5: NaOH (aq) + HCl (aq) → NaCl (aq) + H₂O (l)

Given the above equation, take 45.0 mL of 0.500 M NaOH and neutralize it with a volume of 1.00 M HCl. What's the theoretical volume of HCl needed?

$M_1 = 0.500$ M $\qquad V_1 = 45.0$ mL $\qquad M_2 = 1.00$ M

$M_1V_1 = M_2V_2 \rightarrow V_2 = \frac{M_1V_1}{M_2} \rightarrow V_2 = \frac{(0.500 \text{ M})(45.0 \text{ mL})}{(1.00 \text{ M})} \rightarrow V_2 = \mathbf{22.5 \ mL \ HCl}$

Stoichiometry is needed when the reactants are not one-to-one.

Ex. 6: 3 Ca(OH)₂ (aq) + 2 H₃PO₄ (aq) → Ca₃(PO₄)₂ (s) + 6 H₂O (l)

Given 100. mL of 2.50 M H₃PO₄ to be neutralized by a volume of 0.500 M Ca(OH)₂. Find the volume of Ca(OH)₂ needed. (Recall M is mol/L)

$$(100 \text{ mL}) \left(\frac{1 \text{ L}}{1000 \text{ mL}}\right) \left(\frac{2.50 \text{ mol } H_3PO_4}{1 \text{ L } H_3PO_4}\right) \left(\frac{3 \text{ mol } Ca(OH)_2}{2 \text{ mol } H_3PO_4}\right) \left(\frac{1 \text{ L } Ca(OH)_2}{0.500 \text{ mol } Ca(OH)_2}\right) \left(\frac{1000 \text{ mL}}{L}\right) \rightarrow$$

750 mL of 0.500 M Ca(OH)₂

Thermochemistry

Equations

Kinetic Energy: $\qquad KE = \frac{1}{2}mv^2$

System = heat + work: $\quad \Delta E = q + w$

Heat absorbed by the system (endothermic): $\qquad +q$

Heat released by the system (exothermic): $\qquad -q$

Work done onto the system from surroundings: $\quad +w$

Work done by the system onto the surroundings: $-w$

Work: $\qquad w = -P\Delta V$

Heat: $\qquad q = mC\Delta T \qquad$ ["heat = M-CAT"]

Calorimeter: $\qquad q = C\Delta T \qquad$ ["heat = CAT"]

Enthalpy: $\qquad \Delta H = \sum(Products) - \sum(Reactants)$

Hess's Law: $\qquad$ Elimination Method

Ex. 1: A 250. gram piece of iron at 100. °C is to be doused in a tub containing 400. grams of water at 25. °C. What's the final temperature if the specific heat of iron is 0.444 J / g °C? (Assume no heat is lost to surroundings)

Fe: $\quad$ m = 250. g $\quad$ C = 0.444 J / g °C $\quad \Delta T = x - 100 \qquad$ Note: $\Delta T = T_{final} - T_{initial}$

H_2O: $\quad$ m = 400. g $\quad$ C = 4.184 J / g °C $\quad \Delta T = x - 25$

$q_{H_2O} = -q_{Fe} \rightarrow (H_2O$ gains E$)\ mC\Delta T = -mC\Delta T$ (Fe loses E) $\rightarrow$

$(400.)(4.184)(x - 25.) = -(250.)(0.444)(x - 100.) \rightarrow$

$1673.6(x - 25.) = -111(x - 100.) \rightarrow$

$1673.6x - 41{,}840 = -111x + 11{,}100. \rightarrow$

$1673.6x + 111x = 11{,}100. + 41{,}840 \rightarrow$

$1784.6x = 52{,}940 \rightarrow x = \frac{52{,}940}{1784.6} \rightarrow x = \textbf{29.7 °C}$

Thermochemistry

Ex. 2: A calorimeter is heated up from 20.0 °C to 74.5 °C after a reaction involving 350. grams of substance. The specific heat of the calorimeter is 0.850 J / °C. Find the amount of energy produced per gram of substance.

$$q = C\Delta T \rightarrow q = (0.850)(74.5 - 20.0) \rightarrow q = 46.325 \text{ J}$$

$$\frac{46.325 \text{ J}}{350.\text{g}} \rightarrow \textbf{0.132 J/g}$$

Ex. 3: Find the enthalpy of the following reaction:

C_2H_5OH (l) + 3 O_2 (g) $\rightarrow$ 2 CO_2 (g) + 3 H_2O (l)

Given the following heats of formation:

C_2H_5OH (l) = -276.98 kJ/mol; CO_2 (g) = -393.5 kJ/mol; H_2O (l) = -285.8 kJ/mol

$$\Delta H = \sum(Products) - \sum(Reactants)$$
$$\Delta H = [2(-393.5) + 3(-285.8)] - [(-276.98) + 3(0)]$$
$$\Delta H = -787.0 - 857.4 + 276.98$$
$$\Delta H = \textbf{-1367.4 kJ}$$

Ex. 4: Target: CaO (s) + H_2O (g) $\rightarrow$ Ca(OH)$_2$ (s) $\Delta H = ?$

Given: Ca (s) + $\frac{1}{2}O_2$ (g) $\rightarrow$ CaO (s) $\Delta H = -635.6$ kJ [flip]

H$_2$ (g) + $\frac{1}{2}O_2$ (g) $\rightarrow$ H$_2$O (g) $\Delta H = -241.8$ kJ [flip]

Ca (s) + H$_2$ (g) + O$_2$ (g) $\rightarrow$ Ca(OH)$_2$ (s) $\Delta H = -986.6$ kJ

Modified: CaO (s) $\rightarrow$ Ca (s) + $\frac{1}{2}O_2$ (g) $\Delta H = +635.6$ kJ

H$_2$O (g) $\rightarrow$ H$_2$ (g) + $\frac{1}{2}O_2$ (g) $\Delta H = +241.8$ kJ

Ca (s) + H$_2$ (g) + O$_2$ (g) $\rightarrow$ Ca(OH)$_2$ (s) $\Delta H = -986.6$ kJ

Combined: CaO (s) + H$_2$O (g) $\rightarrow$ Ca(OH)$_2$ (s) $\Delta H = -109.2$ kJ

Solution: **-109.2 kJ**

Modify the given equations to match common compounds within the target.

Basic Quantum Theory

Equations

$$c = \lambda v \qquad v = \frac{c}{\lambda} \qquad \lambda = \frac{c}{v} \qquad \lambda\text{: wavelength} \qquad v\text{: frequency}$$

$$E = hv \qquad v = \frac{E}{h} \qquad E = \frac{hc}{\lambda} \qquad \lambda = \frac{hc}{E} \qquad E\text{: energy}$$

$$E = (-2.178 \cdot 10^{-18})\left(\frac{1}{(n_f)^2} - \frac{1}{(n_i)^2}\right) \quad n_i\text{: initial level} \qquad n_f\text{: final level}$$

Constants: $c = 2.9979 \cdot 10^8$ m/s $\qquad$ Speed of Light

$\qquad\qquad\quad$ $h = 6.626 \cdot 10^{-34}$ J $\cdot$ s $\qquad$ Planck's constant

Visible Spectrum (Approximate)

$\qquad$ (Violet) 400 nm to 750 nm (Red)

Quantum Numbers

$n = 1,2,3,\ldots$
$l = 0,1,\ldots,n-1$
$m_l = -l,\ldots,l$
$m_s = \pm\frac{1}{2}$

l	subshells	m_l & orbitals
0	s	0
1	p	-1 0 1
2	d	-2 -1 0 1 2
3	f	-3 -2 -1 0 1 2 3

Electromagnetic Spectrum

Radio $\qquad\qquad$ [Low Energy / High Wavelength]

Microwave

Infrared

Visible

Ultra Violet

X-Ray

Gamma $\qquad\qquad$ [High Energy / Low Wavelength]

Electron Configuration

1s			1s
2s			2p
3s			3p
4s	3d		4p
5s	4d		5p
6s	5d		6p
7s	6d		7p

4f
5f

Some Exceptions

Cr: [Ar]4s^{1}3d^5 Cu: [Ar]4s^{1}3d^{10}

Mo: [Kr]5s^{1}4d^5 Ag: [Kr]5s^{1}4d^{10}

W: [Xe]6s^{1}4f^{14}5d^5 Au: [Xe]6s^{1}4f^{14}5d^{10}

Quantum Numbers and Electron Configuration

Ex. 1: Find the quantum numbers of the last electron in Co.

Co: 1s^{2}2s^{2}2p^{6}3s^{2}3p^{6}4s^2<u>3d^7</u>

3d → n = 3, l = 2

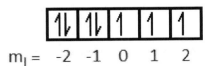

m$_l$ = -2 -1 0 1 2

orbital and spin → m$_l$ = -1, m$_s$ = -½

Last Electron: **(3, 2, -1, -½)**   (n, l, m$_l$, m$_s$)

Electron Configuration

Ex. 2: As: $1s^22s^22p^63s^23p^64s^23d^{10}4p^3$ or $[Ar]4s^23d^{10}4p^3$

   As^{3-}: $1s^22s^22p^63s^23p^64s^23d^{10}4p^6$ or $[Ar]4s^23d^{10}4p^6$

   The negative three charge adds three electrons.

Ex. 3: Fe: $1s^22s^22p^63s^23p^64s^23d^6$ or $[Ar]\ 4s^23d^6$

   Fe^{3+}: $1s^22s^22p^63s^23p^63d^5$ or $[Ar]\ 3d^5$

   The positive three charge removes three electrons.

Ex. 4: Cu: $1s^22s^22p^63s^23p^64s^23d^9$ $\rightarrow$

   Cu: $1s^22s^22p^63s^23p^64s^13d^{10}$ or $[Ar]\ 4s^13d^{10}$

| $4s^23d^9$ | ↑↓ | ↑↓ | ↑↓ | ↑↓ | ↑↓ | ↑ |
| $4s^13d^{10}$ | ↑ | ↑↓ | ↑↓ | ↑↓ | ↑↓ | ↑↓ |

   For this exception, think "eldest child gets their own room."

Ex. 5: Cr: $1s^22s^22p^63s^23p^64s^23d^4$ $\rightarrow$

   Cr: $1s^22s^22p^63s^23p^64s^13d^5$ or $[Ar]\ 4s^13d^5$

| $4s^23d^4$ | ↑↓ | ↑ | ↑ | ↑ | ↑ | |
| $4s^13d^5$ | ↑ | ↑ | ↑ | ↑ | ↑ | ↑ |

   For this exception, think "each child gets their own room."

   The children analogy works for the commonly asked exceptions. Mainly, elements within those groups and sometimes others close by like to rearrange its electrons to gain stability.

   A positive charge will remove electrons from the electron configuration starting with the highest energy level (For instance: 4p, 4s, 3d, 3p, 3s, etc.).

   A negative charge will add electrons to the electron configuration normally.

Periodic Trends and Chemical Bonding

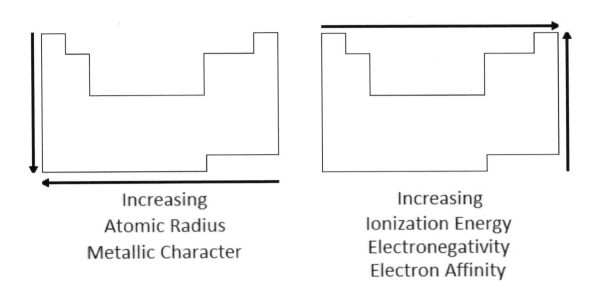

Increasing
Atomic Radius
Metallic Character

Increasing
Ionization Energy
Electronegativity
Electron Affinity

Atomic Radius and Metallic Character increases as one goes to the left and down.
Ionization Energy and Electronegativity increases as one goes to the right and up.
Electron Affinity mostly follows the above trend with several exceptions.

<u>Valence Electrons</u>

1	2	3	4	5	6	7	8
H	He						
Li	Be	B	C	N	O	F	Ne
Na	Mg	Al	Si	P	S	Cl	Ar

<u>Covalent, Ionic, and Metallic Bonding</u>

Nonmetal-Nonmetal:	Covalent Bonding
Metal-Nonmetal:	Ionic Bonding
Metal-Metal:	Metallic Bonding

Periodic Trends and Chemical Bonding

Drawing Lewis Structures

1. Declare the central atom.
   a. "The element that stands out."
   b. "Carbon likes to be the center of attention."
   c. Formally, the least electronegative element. (Mostly)
2. Branch out the other elements.
3. Use Valence Electrons to satisfy the Octet Rule (8 electrons).
   a. Group 1A (Alkali) elements want 2 electrons.
   b. Group 2A (Alkaline Earth) elements want 4 electrons.
   c. Boron and Aluminum want 6 electrons.
   d. Elements in the Transition Metals, elements within 4p to 7p orbitals, P, S, and Cl can exceed the Octet Rule number of electrons.

Polarity

1. Molecular Polarity: From the center, if all electron domains (branches) contain the same element, then the molecule is Nonpolar. Otherwise, if any electron domain is different, then the molecule is Polar. (Use caution with 5 & 6 electron domains and overall Bond Polarities.)
2. Bond Polarity: Difference of Electronegativity
   a. Less than 0.5:   Nonpolar
   b. Between 0.5 and 2.0:   Polar Covalent
   c. More than 2.0:   Polar Ionic

Bonding Energy

$$\Delta H(bonding) = \sum(Reactant\ Bonds) - \sum(Product\ Bonds)$$

For the above formula, draw the Lewis Dot Structures and count the number of bonds. One should keep in mind the coefficients of the molecules within the chemical equation.

Molecular and Electron Geometry

Electron Domains	Lone Pairs	Molecular Geometry	VSPER
2	0	Linear	AX_2
3	0	Trigonal Planar	AX_3
	1	Bent (V-Shaped)	AX_2E
4	0	Tetrahedral	AX_4
	1	Trigonal Pyramidal	AX_3E
	2	Bent (V-Shaped)	AX_2E_2
5	0	Trigonal Bipyramidal	AX_5
	1	See-Saw	AX_4E
	2	T-Shaped	AX_3E_2
	3	Linear	AX_2E_3
6	0	Octahedral	AX_6
	1	Square Pyramidal	AX_5E
	2	Square Planar	AX_4E_2

Electron Domains	Electron Geometry	Bond Angles	Hybridization
2	Linear	180°	sp
3	Trigonal Planar	120°	sp^2
4	Tetrahedral	109.5°	sp^3
5	Trigonal Bipyramidal	90°, 120°	
6	Octahedral	90°	

Note: The bond angles are approximate for the above table. Hybridizations with the 5 and 6 electron domains were theoretically designated as sp^3d and sp^3d^2 respectively.

Molecular and Electron Geometry

3D Models

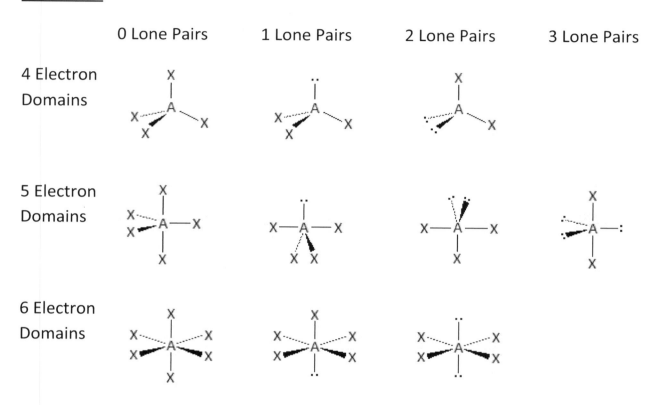

Author's Note: Some Chemistry professors may have a preferred set of 3D illustrations for students to follow that may differ from the above illustrations. In that regard, please adapt to the professor's preference.

Bond Order and Magnetic Properties

	B$_2$	C$_2$	N$_2$	O$_2$	F$_2$	Ne$_2$
σ 2p*						↑↓
π 2p*				↑ ↑	↑↓ ↑↓	↑↓ ↑↓
σ 2p			↑↓	↑↓	↑↓	↑↓
π 2p	↑ ↑	↑↓ ↑↓	↑↓ ↑↓	↑↓ ↑↓	↑↓ ↑↓	↑↓ ↑↓
σ 2s*	↑↓	↑↓	↑↓	↑↓	↑↓	↑↓
σ 2s	↑↓	↑↓	↑↓	↑↓	↑↓	↑↓
Bond Order	1	2	3	2	1	0
Magnetic Properties	Paramagnetic	Diamagnetic	Diamagnetic	Paramagnetic	Diamagnetic	None

Bond Order Calculation

$$[Bond\ Order] = \frac{[Bonding\ Electrons] - [Antibonding\ Electrons]}{2}$$

Magnetic Properties

Paramagnetic: Non-countered electron spin. (Has unpaired electrons)

Diamagnetic: Countered electron spin. (Has no unpaired electrons)

Sigma and Pi Bonds

Bond Type	Sigma (σ) Bonds	Pi (π) Bonds
Single Bond:	1 σ-bond	0 π-bonds
Double Bond:	1 σ-bond	1 π-bond
Triple Bond:	1 σ-bond	2 π-bonds

Gas Laws

Equations

$$\frac{P_1 V_1}{n_1 T_1} = \frac{P_2 V_2}{n_2 T_2}$$ (Eliminate variables that are constant. T in K)

$$PV = nRT$$ (P in atm, V in L, n in mol, and T in K. R = 0.08206 L atm / mol K)

$$d = \frac{PM}{RT}$$ (P in atm, M in g/mol, T in K. R = 0.08206 L atm / mol K)

$$X_i = \frac{n_i}{n_{total}} = \frac{P_i}{P_{total}}$$ (Mole Fraction)

$$u_{rms} = \sqrt{\frac{3RT}{M}}$$ (R = 8.314 J / mol K, T in K, M in kg/mol)

$$\frac{r_1}{r_2} = \sqrt{\frac{M_2}{M_1}}$$ (r in g/s or mL/s and M in g/mol)

Author's Note: Gas Laws require knowledge of algebraic manipulation in order to ingest the equations more properly. In fact, like any other Math oriented class, Chemistry requires students to practice the concepts vigorously.

Ex. 1: A balloon initially contains a volume of 5.0 L of an ideal gas at a temperature of 25.0 °C. If the balloon is cooled to 10.0 °C, what would be the new volume of the balloon? (Pressure and moles of gas are constant.)

$$V_1 = 5.0 \text{ L} \qquad T_1 = 25.0 \text{ C} \rightarrow 298.15 \text{ K} \qquad T_2 = 10.0 \text{ C} \rightarrow 283.15 \text{ K}$$

$$\frac{P_1 V_1}{n_1 T_1} = \frac{P_2 V_2}{n_2 T_2} \rightarrow \frac{V_1}{T_1} = \frac{V_2}{T_2} \rightarrow V_2 = \frac{V_1 T_2}{T_1} \rightarrow V_2 = \frac{(5.0 \text{ L})(283.15 \text{ K})}{(298.15 \text{ K})} \rightarrow \mathbf{4.7 \text{ L}}$$

Gas Laws

Ex. 2: Given 750.0 g of C_3H_8 at 20.0 °C and contained in a volume of 25.0 L, what would be the pressure exerted inside the container? (Molar Mass: 44.094 g/mol)

$V = 25.0 \text{ L}$ $T = 20.0 \text{ C} \rightarrow 293.15 \text{ K}$

$n = (750.0 \text{ g}) \left(\frac{\text{mol}}{44.094 \text{ g}} \right) \rightarrow 17.01 \text{ mol}$

$PV = nRT \rightarrow P = \frac{nRT}{V} \rightarrow P = \frac{(17.01 \text{ mol})(0.08206 \frac{\text{L atm}}{\text{mol K}})(293.15 \text{ K})}{(25.0 \text{ L})} \rightarrow \mathbf{16.4 \text{ atm}}$

Ex. 3: If 200.0 g of Cl_2 is contained to a pressure of 71.5 inHg and a volume of 100.0 in³, what would be the temperature of the container? (Molar Mass: 70.90 g/mol)

$n = (200.0 \text{ g}) \left(\frac{\text{mol}}{70.90 \text{ g}} \right) \rightarrow 2.821 \text{ mol } Cl_2$

$P = (71.5 \text{ inHg}) \left(\frac{25.4 \text{ mmHg}}{\text{inHg}} \right) \left(\frac{\text{atm}}{760 \text{ mmHg}} \right) \rightarrow 2.39 \text{ atm}$

$V = (100.0 \text{ in}^3) \left(\frac{16.387064 \text{ cm}^3}{\text{in}^3} \right) \left(\frac{\text{L}}{1000 \text{ cm}^3} \right) \rightarrow 1.639 \text{ L}$

$PV = nRT \rightarrow T = \frac{PV}{nR} \rightarrow T = \frac{(2.39 \text{ atm})(1.639 \text{ L})}{(2.821 \text{ mol})(0.08206 \frac{\text{L atm}}{\text{mol K}})} \rightarrow \mathbf{16.9 \text{ K}}$

Ex. 4: Find the density of CO_2 under a pressure of 1.25 atm at a temperature of 295.15 K. (Molar Mass: 44.01 g/mol)

$P = 1.25 \text{ atm}$ $M = 44.01 \text{ g/mol}$ $T = 295.15 \text{ K}$

$d = \frac{PM}{RT} \rightarrow d = \frac{(1.25 \text{ atm})(44.01 \text{ g/mol})}{(0.08206 \frac{\text{L atm}}{\text{mol K}})(295.15 \text{ K})} \rightarrow \mathbf{2.27 \text{ g/L}}$

Gas Laws

Ex. 5: Find the molar mass of an ideal gas if the density is 5.74 g/L, the pressure is 2.40 atm, and the temperature of 25.0 °C.

$$d = 5.74 \text{ g/L} \qquad T = 25.0 \text{ C} \rightarrow 298.15 \text{ K} \qquad P = 2.40 \text{ atm}$$

$$d = \frac{PM}{RT} \rightarrow dRT = PM \rightarrow M = \frac{dRT}{P} \rightarrow M = \frac{(5.74 \text{ g/L})(0.08206 \frac{\text{L atm}}{\text{mol K}})(298.15 \text{ K})}{(2.40 \text{ atm})} \rightarrow$$

58.5 g/mol

Ex. 6: Find the root-mean-squared (rms) of C_4H_{10} at a temperature of 45.0 °C. (Molar Mass: 58.12 g/mol)

$$T = 45.0 \text{ C} \rightarrow 318.15 \text{ K} \qquad M = 58.12 \text{ g/mol} \rightarrow 0.05812 \text{ kg/mol}$$

$$u_{rms} = \sqrt{\frac{3RT}{M}} \rightarrow u_{rms} = \sqrt{\frac{3(8.314 \frac{\text{J}}{\text{mol K}})(318.15 \text{ K})}{(0.05812 \text{ kg/mol})}} \rightarrow \textbf{369.5 m/s}$$

Ex. 7: If O_2 diffuses at a rate of 20.0 g/s, then what rate would Cl_2 diffuse? (Molar Mass of O_2: 32.00 g/mol; Molar Mass of Cl_2: 70.90 g/mol)

$$r_1 = 20.0 \text{ g/s} \qquad M_1 = 32.00 \text{ g/mol} \qquad M_2 = 70.90 \text{ g/mol}$$

$$\frac{r_1}{r_2} = \sqrt{\frac{M_2}{M_1}} \rightarrow \frac{r_2}{r_1} = \sqrt{\frac{M_1}{M_2}} \rightarrow r_2 = r_1\sqrt{\frac{M_1}{M_2}} \rightarrow r_2 = (20.0 \text{ g/s})\sqrt{\frac{(32.00 \text{ g/mol})}{(70.90 \text{ g/mol})}} \rightarrow$$

13.4 g/s

Standard Temperature and Pressure (STP): 1 atm, 273.15 K, 1 mol = 22.414 L

Physical Properties of Liquids and Solids – Intermolecular Forces

Intermolecular Forces

1. London Dispersion: All Molecules
2. Dipole-Dipole: Polar Molecules
3. Hydrogen Bonding: H^+ bonded with N, O, or F
4. Ion-Dipole: Metal-Nonmetal

Phase Conversions

Solid	→	Liquid	=	Melting
Liquid	→	Gas	=	Vaporization
Solid	→	Gas	=	Sublimation
Gas	→	Liquid	=	Condensation
Liquid	→	Solid	=	Freezing
Gas	→	Solid	=	Deposition

Phase Diagram

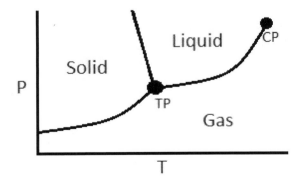

TP: Triple Point (All three states)
CP: Critical Point (Phase beyond this point: Supercritical fluid)

Physical Properties of Liquids and Solids – Intermolecular Forces

Clausius–Clapeyron Equation

$$\ln\left(\frac{P_1}{P_2}\right) = \frac{\Delta H_{vap}}{R}\left(\frac{1}{T_2} - \frac{1}{T_1}\right) \qquad R = 8.314\frac{J}{mol\ K}$$

Ex. 1: Given that H_2O has a vapor pressure of 31.82 mmHg at 30.0 °C, what will the vapor pressure be at 75.0 °C? (Enthalpy of vaporization: 40.79 kJ/mol)

$\Delta H_{vap} = 40.79$ kJ/mol $\rightarrow$ 40,790 J/mol $\qquad T_1 = 303.15$ K $\qquad T_2 = 348.15$ K

$$\ln\left(\frac{P_1}{P_2}\right) = \frac{\Delta H_{vap}}{R}\left(\frac{1}{T_2} - \frac{1}{T_1}\right) \rightarrow \ln\left(\frac{31.82}{P_2}\right) = \frac{40,790}{8.314}\left(\frac{1}{348.15} - \frac{1}{303.15}\right) \rightarrow$$

$\ln(31.82) - \ln P_2 = -2.091858 \rightarrow -\ln P_2 = -2.091858 - \ln(31.82) \rightarrow$

$\ln P_2 = 5.551953 \rightarrow P_2 = e^{5.551953} \rightarrow$ **258 mmHg**

Unit Cell

Atom Position	Fraction of Atom
Center	1
Face	1 / 2
Edge	1 / 4
Corner	1 / 8

Primitive Cell	= 1 atom	$a = 2r$
Body-Centered	= 2 atoms	$a = \frac{4}{\sqrt{3}}r$
Face-Centered	= 4 atoms	$a = 2\sqrt{2}r$

a = side of the cell

r = atomic radius

Physical Properties of Liquids and Solids – Intermolecular Forces

Energy required in converting phases of matter

Ex. 2: Cody and Kevin want to boil some ice. Such curiosity to wonder where the ice goes once heated. How much total energy is required to vaporize 125.0 grams of ice at − 10.00 °C to 120.00 °C? (Molar Mass: 18.016 g/mol)

Specific Heat of Ice: 2.092 J / g K
Specific Heat of water: 4.184 J / g K
Specific Heat of steam: 1.841 J / g K
Heat of fusion: 6.008 kJ/mol
Heat of vaporization: 40.67 kJ/mol
Melting Point: 0.00 °C
Boiling Point: 100.00 °C

Phase 1:   Ice (− 10.00 °C)   →   Ice (0.00 °C)

$$q = mC\Delta T \rightarrow q = (125.0 \text{ g})(2.092 \tfrac{J}{g \, K})(10.00 \text{ °C}) \rightarrow 2615 \text{ J} \rightarrow 2.615 \text{ kJ}$$

Phase 2:   Ice   →   Water

$$(125.0 \text{ g})\left(\tfrac{\text{mol}}{18.016 \text{ g}}\right)(6.008 \text{ kJ/mol}) \rightarrow 41.69 \text{ kJ}$$

Phase 3:   Water (0.00 °C)   →   Water (100.00 °C)

$$q = mC\Delta T \rightarrow q = (125.0 \text{ g})(4.184 \tfrac{J}{g \, K})(100.00 \text{ °C}) \rightarrow 52300 \text{ J} \rightarrow 52.30 \text{ kJ}$$

Phase 4:   Water   →   Steam

$$(125.0 \text{ g})\left(\tfrac{\text{mol}}{18.016 \text{ g}}\right)(40.67 \text{ kJ/mol}) \rightarrow 282.2 \text{ kJ}$$

Phase 5:   Steam (100.00 °C)   →   Steam (120.00 °C)

$$q = mC\Delta T \rightarrow q = (125.0 \text{ g})(1.841 \tfrac{J}{g \, K})(20.00 \text{ °C}) \rightarrow 4603 \text{ J} \rightarrow 4.603 \text{ kJ}$$

Total: 2.615 kJ + 41.69 kJ + 52.30 kJ + 282.2 kJ + 4.603 kJ = **383.4 kJ**

Physical Properties of Solutions

Molality (m)

$$m = \frac{\text{moles of solute}}{\text{kg of solvent}}$$

Solute: the lesser amount of the two solutions (Unless stated otherwise)
Solvent: the greater amount of the two solutions (Unless stated otherwise)

Vapor Pressure involving Solution

$$P_i = X_i P_0 \qquad X_i: \text{mol fraction} \qquad P_0: \text{initial pressure}$$

Freezing Point (FP) and Boiling Point (BP)

$$FP_f = FP_i - \Delta T_f \qquad\qquad FP_f: \text{final freezing point}$$
$$\Delta T_f = k_f m \qquad\qquad\qquad FP_i: \text{initial freezing point}$$
$$k: \text{freezing or boiling constant}$$
$$BP_f = BP_i + \Delta T_b \qquad\qquad BP_f: \text{final boiling point}$$
$$\Delta T_b = k_b m \qquad\qquad\qquad BP_i: \text{initial boiling point}$$

Ex. 1: Given 100.0 gram of H_2O and add 27.02 grams of $C_6H_{12}O_6$ (180.156 g/mol), find the freezing and boiling points of the solution. ($k_f = 1.86\,°C/m$, $k_b = 0.512\,°C/m$)

$$(27.02 \text{ g } C_6H_{12}O_6)\left(\frac{\text{mol } C_6H_{12}O_6}{180.156 \text{ g } C_6H_{12}O_6}\right) \rightarrow 0.1500 \text{ mol } C_6H_{12}O_6$$
$$m = \frac{0.1500 \text{ mol } C_6H_{12}O_6}{0.1000 \text{ kg}} \rightarrow 1.500 \, m \, C_6H_{12}O_6$$

$\Delta T_f = k_f m \rightarrow (1.86)(1.500) \rightarrow 2.79$ $\qquad$ $\Delta T_b = k_b m \rightarrow (0.512)(1.500) \rightarrow 0.78$

$FP_f = FP_i - \Delta T_f \rightarrow 0.00 - 2.79$ $\qquad$ $BP_f = BP_i + \Delta T_b \rightarrow 100.00 + 0.78$

$FP_f = \mathbf{-2.79\,°C}$ $\qquad\qquad\qquad$ $BP_f = \mathbf{100.78\,°C}$

Physical Properties of Solutions

Osmotic Pressure

$$\pi = MRT \quad (M\text{: Molarity}, R = 0.08206 \frac{\text{L atm}}{\text{mol K}}, T \text{ in K})$$

Van't Hoff factor (i)

$$\Delta T_f = ik_f m \qquad \qquad \Delta T_b = ik_b m \qquad \qquad \pi = iMRT$$

Essentially, whenever the solution contains ions from the complete dissociation of the solute (Strong Electrolyte).

$i = \#$ of ions in solution [Integer] (Unless stated directly)

Ex. 2: Leni, Logan, Levi, Cody, Madison, Kevin, and Stefin want to make some ice cream. With the aid of plastic bags and protective gloves (as the icy solution in this experiment will become very cold!), place the icy water and salt into one bag and a double bagged amount of ice cream mix in liquid form in another. After some shaking, the icy solution will get much cooler and eventually freeze the ice cream inside. What's the freezing point of the icy solution containing 250.0 grams of icy water and 6 oz of salt? ($k_f = 1.86\,°C/m$; Molar Mass: 58.44 g/mol)

$$(6 \text{ oz NaCl}) \left(\frac{28.3 \text{ g NaCl}}{\text{oz NaCl}}\right) \left(\frac{\text{mol NaCl}}{58.44 \text{ g NaCl}}\right) \rightarrow 2.90554 \text{ mol NaCl}$$

$$m = \frac{2.90554 \text{ mol NaCl}}{0.2500 \text{ kg}} \rightarrow 11.6222 \, m \text{ NaCl}$$

NaCl (aq) → Na⁺ (aq) + Cl⁻ (aq) $\qquad \qquad i = 2$

$$\Delta T_f = ik_f m \rightarrow (2)(1.86\,°C/m)(11.6222 \, m) \rightarrow 43.2\,°C$$

$$FP_f = FP_i - \Delta T_f \rightarrow 0.00 - 43.2 \rightarrow \mathbf{-43.2\,°C}$$

Electrolytes

Strong Electrolytes (Completely breaks down into ions)

1. Strong Acids: HCl, $HClO_3$, $HClO_4$, HBr, $HBrO_3$, $HBrO_4$, HI, HIO_3, HIO_4, H_2SO_4, H_2SeO_4, H_2TeO_4, HNO_3
2. Strong Bases: $LiOH$, $NaOH$, KOH, $CsOH$, $RbOH$, $Ca(OH)_2$, $Ba(OH)_2$, $Sr(OH)_2$
3. Completely Soluble

Solubility Rules (Greater Detail):

Always Soluble: Alkali, NH_4^+, NO_3^-, $C_2H_3O_2^-$, ClO_3^-, ClO_4^-, BrO_3^-, BrO_4^-, IO_3^-, IO_4^-

Mostly Soluble: Cl^-, Br^-, I^- (except w/ Ag^+, Hg_2^{2+}, Pb^{2+})

SO_4^{2-}, SeO_4^{2-}, TeO_4^{2-} (except w/ Ca^{2+}, Sr^{2+}, Ba^{2+}, Hg^{2+}, Pb^{2+})

Mostly Insoluble: OH^- (except w/ Ca^{2+}, Sr^{2+}, Ba^{2+})

CO_3^{2-}, $C_2O_4^{2-}$, PO_4^{3-}, AsO_4^{3-}, CrO_4^{2-}, SO_3^{2-}, SeO_3^{2-}, TeO_3^{2-}, NO_2^-, S^{2-}, F^-, CN^-, OCN^-, SCN^-

Other anions ending in –ite or –ide

(*$CaSO_4$ is considered within a middle ground between soluble and insoluble.)

Weak Electrolytes (Partially breaks down into ions)

1. Weak Acids: All other acids   (This includes Acetic Acid: $HC_2H_3O_2$)
2. Weak Bases: All other bases (This includes Ammonia: NH_3)
3. Slightly Soluble

Non-electrolytes (Does not break down into ions)

1. Molecular Compounds

Kinetics

Equations

a A + b B → c C + d D

$$rate = -\frac{1}{a} \cdot \frac{\Delta[A]}{\Delta t} = -\frac{1}{b} \cdot \frac{\Delta[B]}{\Delta t} = \frac{1}{c} \cdot \frac{\Delta[C]}{\Delta t} = \frac{1}{d} \cdot \frac{\Delta[D]}{\Delta t}$$

$$rate = k[A]^m[B]^n$$

$$\frac{rate_1}{rate_2} = \frac{k[A_1]^m[B_1]^n}{k[A_2]^m[B_2]^n}$$

First Order Reactions ($rate = k[A]^1$)

$$\ln[A_t] = -kt + \ln[A_0]$$

$$t_{\frac{1}{2}} = \frac{\ln 2}{k} \qquad \text{(half-life)}$$

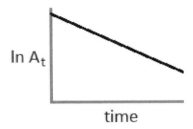

Second Order Reactions ($rate = k[A]^2$)

$$\frac{1}{[A_t]} = kt + \frac{1}{[A_0]}$$

$$t_{\frac{1}{2}} = \frac{1}{k[A_0]} \qquad \text{(half-life)}$$

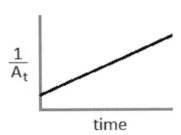

Reactions Involving Temperature and Collisions

$$k = Ae^{\left(-\frac{E_a}{RT}\right)} \qquad A: \text{Collision frequency}$$

$$\ln k = \left(-\frac{E_a}{R}\right)\left(\frac{1}{T}\right) + \ln A \qquad E_a: \text{Activation Energy}$$

$$\ln\left(\frac{k_1}{k_2}\right) = \left(-\frac{E_a}{R}\right)\left(\frac{1}{T_1} - \frac{1}{T_2}\right) \qquad R = 8.314 \frac{J}{\text{mol K}}$$

$$T: \text{Temperature in Kelvin}$$

Equilibrium Basics

Concentration and Equilibrium Constant

$$a A + b B \longleftrightarrow c C + d D$$

$$K_c = \frac{[C]^c[D]^d}{[A]^a[B]^b}$$

Equilibrium Shift

1. Adding or Removing a substance
   a. Shift Right: Adding reactant or Removing product
   b. Shift Left: Removing reactant or Adding product
2. Change in Volume and Pressure
   a. Volume Increases (Pressure Decreases): Reaction shifts towards the side with the higher amount of moles of gas.
   b. Volume Decreases (Pressure Increases): Reaction shifts towards the side with the lower amount of moles of gas.
3. Change in Temperature (Endothermic and Exothermic)
   a. Increasing Temp: Endothermic (Shift Right), Exothermic (Shift Left)
   b. Decreasing Temp: Endothermic (Shift Left), Exothermic (Shift Right)

Relation between Concentration and Pressure Constants

$$K_p = K_c(RT)^{\Delta n} \qquad\qquad (0.08206 \frac{\text{L atm}}{\text{mol K}})$$

$$\Delta n = moles\ of\ gas\ (product) - moles\ of\ gas\ (reactant)$$

Acids and Bases

Definitions

Brønsted-Lowry Acids: Proton Donor   (H^+ or H_3O^+ commonly)

Brønsted-Lowry Bases: Proton Acceptor (OH^- commonly)

Lewis Acids: Electron Pair Acceptor

Lewis Bases: Electron Pair Donors

Conjugate Base: Remains of the Acid after neutralization

Conjugate Acid: Remains of the Base after neutralization

pH Scale and pH equations

Acidic: pH < 6.5   Neutral: 6.5 < pH < 7.5   Basic: pH > 7.5

$$pH = -\log[H_3O^+]$$

$$pOH = -\log[OH^-]$$

$$[H_3O^+] = 10^{-pH}$$

$$[OH^-] = 10^{-pOH}$$

$$pH = 14 - pOH$$

$$pOH = 14 - pH$$

Water

H_2O (l)   + H_2O (l)   ⟷ OH^- (aq)   + H_3O^+ (aq)

[Acid]   [Base]   [Conjugate Base] [Conjugate Acid]

$$K_w = [H_3O^+][OH^-] = 1.0 \cdot 10^{-14} \text{ (at 25.0 }^\circ\text{C)}$$

$$K_a \cdot K_b = K_w$$

Acids and Bases

Multiple Ionizations of H^+ (Diprotic and Polyprotic Acids)

Ex. 1: $H_2SO_4 \rightarrow HSO_4^- + H^+$ $K_a = Very\ Large$

        $HSO_4^- \rightarrow SO_4^{2-} + H^+$ $K_a = 1.3 \cdot 10^{-2}$

Ex. 2: $H_3PO_4 \rightarrow H_2PO_4^- + H^+$ $K_a = 7.5 \cdot 10^{-3}$

        $H_2PO_4^- \rightarrow HPO_4^{2-} + H^+$ $K_a = 6.2 \cdot 10^{-8}$

        $HPO_4^{2-} \rightarrow PO_4^{3-} + H^+$ $K_a = 4.2 \cdot 10^{-13}$

Acid-Base Properties of Salt Solution Situations

1. Makes a Solution Acidic:

    Conjugate Acid of a Weak Base with H_2O

    Metal Ions of Weak Electrolytes with H_2O

2. Makes a Solution Basic:

    Conjugate Base of a Weak Acid with H_2O

3. No effect to Solution:

    Ions of Strong Electrolytes (Conjugate Acids of Strong Bases, Conjugate Bases of Strong Acids, and Metal Ions of Strong Electrolytes)

Acid-Base Properties of Oxides

     Metal Oxides + Water $\rightarrow$ Bases

     Nonmetal Oxides + Water $\rightarrow$ Acids

Ex. 3: $CaO + H_2O \rightarrow Ca(OH)_2$

Ex. 4: $SO_3 + H_2O \rightarrow H_2SO_4$

Acids and Bases

Equilibrium of Acids and Bases

Ex. 5: Find the pH of a 0.500 M $HC_2H_3O_2$ once the solution reaches equilibrium. $(K_a = 1.8 \cdot 10^{-5})$

First, express the chemical equation with an "ICE" table:

	$HC_2H_3O_2$	$\longleftrightarrow$	H^+	+	$C_2H_3O_2^-$
I	0.500 M		0 M		0 M
C	$-x$		$+x$		$+x$
E	$0.500 - x$		x		x

Add x to the side of the equation with initial values of zero, and subtract x from the other side of the equation. This is the amount shifted to reach equilibrium.

Second, construct an equilibrium equation (K_a):

$$K_a = \frac{[H^+][C_2H_3O_2^-]}{[HC_2H_3O_2]} \rightarrow 1.8 \cdot 10^{-5} = \frac{(x)(x)}{(0.500-x)} \rightarrow 1.8 \cdot 10^{-5} = \frac{(x)(x)}{(0.5)}$$

One can omit the addition or subtraction of 'x' since its value would be insignificant compared to the constant next to it.

$$\frac{x^2}{0.5} = 1.8 \cdot 10^{-5} \rightarrow x^2 = 9.0 \cdot 10^{-6} \rightarrow x = 3.0 \cdot 10^{-3}$$

Finally, plug in the concentration of H^+ into the pH equation:

$$pH = -\log[3.0 \cdot 10^{-3}] \rightarrow pH = \mathbf{2.52}$$

Author's Note: Alternately, instead of omitting the x from the second step above, we could have simplified the equation and set it equal to zero. Then we could have used the quadratic formula to solve for x. This method is more accurate, but if the value of x is very low (K value involved is less than 1/1000 of the initial concentration) then the increase in accuracy would be negligible. In fact, the quadratic formula would have yielded the same value or a value very close to the one obtained using the omission method above.

Acids and Bases

The "ICE" box stands for Initial, Change, and Equilibrium. The first row contains the starting values of the equilibrium equation. The second row contains the change in concentration to get to equilibrium. If no amount is specified as the concentration change, then assume the value 'x' as the unknown (the coefficient of 'x' is the same as the substance in the chemical equation in the same column). The third row contains the final concentrations of the substances at equilibrium.

Also, the significant figures for pH and pOH are separate from the usual rule set for significant figures. The number for pH and pOH will contain a number of decimal places equal to the significant figures of the concentration of H^+, H_3O^+, or OH^-.

Acid-Base and Solubility Equilibrium

Henderson-Hasselbach Equation (pH of a Buffer)

$$pH = pK_a + \log\left(\frac{[A^-]}{[HA]}\right) \qquad pK_a = -\log(K_a)$$

$[A^-]$: Conjugate Base $\qquad\qquad$ $[HA]$: Weak Acid

Other Concepts

K_{sp} : Solubility Product Constant

K_f : Formation Constant (Complex Ions)

Common Ion Effect: Add initial values to substances effected

Ex. 1: Find the pH of the mixture of 50.0 mL of 0.200 M HCl and 25.0 mL of 0.150 M LiOH.

$(0.200 \text{ M HCl})(50.0 \text{ mL}) \rightarrow 10.0 \text{ mmol HCl}$
$(0.150 \text{ M LiOH})(25.0 \text{ mL}) \rightarrow 3.75 \text{ mmol LiOH}$

	HCl (aq) +	LiOH (aq) →	LiCl (aq) +	H$_2$O (l)
I	10.0	3.75	0	0
C	-3.75	-3.75	+3.75	+3.75
F	6.25	0	3.75	3.75

Since HCl is a strong acid, the H$^+$ ions will dissociate completely.

$\dfrac{6.25 \text{ mmol}}{75.0 \text{ mL}} \rightarrow 0.0833 \text{ M H}^+ \qquad pH = -\log(0.0833) \rightarrow \mathbf{pH = 1.08}$

Acid-Base and Solubility Equilibrium

Ex. 2: Find the pH of 20.0 mL of 0.200 M C_6H_5OH and 10.0 mL of 0.100 M NaOH. ($K_a = 1.3 \cdot 10^{-10}$)

$$(0.200 \text{ M } C_6H_5OH)(20.0 \text{ mL}) \rightarrow 4.00 \text{ mmol } C_6H_5OH$$
$$(0.100 \text{ M NaOH})(10.0 \text{ mL}) \rightarrow 1.00 \text{ mmol NaOH}$$

	C_6H_5OH (aq) +	NaOH (aq) $\rightarrow$	H_2O (l) +	C_6H_5ONa (aq)
I	4.00	1.00	0	0
C	-1.00	-1.00	+1.00	+1.00
F	3.00	0	1.00	1.00

$$\frac{3.00 \text{ mmol}}{30.0 \text{ mL}} \rightarrow 0.100 \text{ M } C_6H_5OH \qquad \frac{1.00 \text{ mmol}}{30.0 \text{ mL}} \rightarrow 0.0333 \text{ M } C_6H_5O^-$$

	C_6H_5OH (aq) $\leftrightarrow$	H^+ (aq) +	$C_6H_5O^-$ (aq)
I	0.100 M	0 M	0.0333 M
C	$-x$	$+x$	$+x$
E	$0.100 - x$	x	$x + 0.0333$

$$K_a = \frac{[H^+][C_6H_5O^-]}{[HC_6H_5O]} \rightarrow 1.3 \cdot 10^{-10} = \frac{(x)(x+0.0333)}{(0.100-x)} \rightarrow 1.3 \cdot 10^{-10} = \frac{(x)(0.0333)}{(0.100)}$$

$$0.333x = 1.3 \cdot 10^{-10} \rightarrow x = 3.9 \cdot 10^{-10}$$

$$pH = -\log(3.9 \cdot 10^{-10}) \rightarrow pH = \mathbf{9.41}$$

Author's Note: The ICF Table above represents the Initial, Change, and Final values within the initial reaction. Keep in mind of the coefficients of the compounds within the chemical formula. The coefficients will alter the change values by a factor equal to itself within each respective compound. Also, the ICE Table requires the values plugged in to be in the form of concentration. So after the ICF Table calculation, divide the values obtained by the total volume to obtain the concentration of each compound involved.

Acid-Base and Solubility Equilibrium

Ex. 3: Find pH of the mixture of 75.0 mL of 0.150 M $C_2H_5NH_2$ ($K_b = 5.6 \cdot 10^{-4}$) and 25.0 mL of 0.100 M $HClO_4$.

$$(0.150 \text{ M } C_2H_5NH_2)(75.0 \text{ mL}) \rightarrow 11.25 \text{ mmol } C_2H_5NH_2$$
$$(0.100 \text{ M } HClO_4)(25.0 \text{ mL}) \rightarrow 2.50 \text{ mmol } HClO_4$$

	$C_2H_5NH_2$ (aq) +	$HClO_4$ (aq) →	ClO_4^- (aq) +	$C_2H_5NH_3^+$ (aq)
I	11.25	2.50	0	0
C	-2.50	-2.50	+2.50	+2.50
F	8.75	0	2.50	2.50

$$\frac{8.75 \text{ mmol}}{100.0 \text{ mL}} \rightarrow 0.0875 \text{ M } C_2H_5NH_2 \qquad \frac{2.50 \text{ mmol}}{100.0 \text{ mL}} \rightarrow 0.0250 \text{ M } C_2H_5NH_3^+$$

	$C_2H_5NH_2$ (aq) +	H_2O (l) ←→	OH^- (aq) +	$C_2H_5NH_3^+$ (aq)
I	0.0875 M	--	0 M	0.0250 M
C	$-x$	--	$+x$	$+x$
E	$0.0875 - x$	--	x	$x + 0.0250$

$K_b = \frac{[OH^-][C_2H_5NH_3^+]}{[C_2H_5NH_2]} \rightarrow 5.6 \cdot 10^{-4} = \frac{(x)(x+0.0250)}{(0.0875-x)} \rightarrow$
$5.6 \cdot 10^{-4}(0.0875 - x) = (x)(x + 0.0250) \rightarrow$
$4.9 \cdot 10^{-5} - (5.6 \cdot 10^{-4})x = x^2 + 0.0250x \rightarrow$
$x^2 + 0.02556x - 4.9 \cdot 10^{-5} = 0$

$$x = \frac{-(0.02556)+\sqrt{(0.02556)^2-4(1)(-4.9\cdot10^{-5})}}{2(1)} \rightarrow x = 0.00179 \text{ M } OH^-$$

$pOH = -\log(0.00179) \rightarrow pOH = 2.75$

$pH = 14 - pOH \rightarrow pH = 14 - 2.75 \rightarrow pH = \mathbf{11.25}$

Entropy and Free Energy

Entropy

ΔS increases with disorder. (Solids → Liquids → Gases; Less → More)

$S = k \ln W$ $\qquad k = 1.38 \cdot 10^{-23}$ J/K

$W = n^x$ $\qquad n$: Possible positions $\qquad x$: Number of molecules

$\Delta S_{rxn} = \sum(Products) - \sum(Reactants)$

$\Delta S_{surroundings} = -\dfrac{\Delta H_{system}}{T}$ $\qquad$ (T in Kelvin)

Gibb's Free Energy

$\Delta G = \Delta H - T\Delta S$ $\qquad \Delta G < 0$ $\qquad$ Spontaneous

$\qquad\qquad\qquad\qquad \Delta G > 0$ $\qquad$ Nonspontaneous

$\qquad\qquad\qquad\qquad \Delta G = 0$ $\qquad$ System at Equilibrium

ΔH	ΔS	T	ΔG
+	−		+
−	+		−
+	+	High	−
+	+	Low	+
−	−	High	+
−	−	Low	−

$\Delta G° = \sum(Products) - \sum(Reactants)$

$\Delta G = \Delta G° + RT \ln Q$ $\qquad (R = 8.314 \cdot 10^{-3} \frac{kJ}{mol\,K}$, Q: Reactant Quotient)

$\Delta G° = -RT \ln K$ $\qquad$ (K: Equilibrium Constant, $\Delta G = 0$, $Q = K$)

Other Concepts within Chemistry

Electrochemical Equations

$$E°_{cell} = E°_{cathode} - E°_{anode}$$

Anode: where oxidation occurs (draws in anions)

Cathode: where reduction occurs (draws in cations)

$$\Delta G = -nFE_{cell}$$

$$F = 96{,}485 \frac{J}{V \text{ (moles electrons)}} \quad \text{(Faraday)}$$

$$n = number\ of\ moles\ of\ electrons$$

$$E°_{cell} = \frac{RT}{nF} \ln K$$

$$R = 8.314 \frac{J}{mol\ K}$$

K: Equilibrium Constant

$$E = E°_{cell} - \frac{RT}{nF} \ln Q$$

Q: Reaction Quotient

Basic Nuclear Chemistry

Proton: $\quad {}_{1}^{1}H^{+}$ or ${}_{1}^{1}p$

Neutron: $\quad {}_{0}^{1}n$

Electron (Negative Beta particle): $\quad {}_{-1}^{0}e$ or ${}_{-1}^{0}\beta^{-}$

Positron (Positive Beta particle): $\quad {}_{1}^{0}e$ or ${}_{1}^{0}\beta^{+}$

Alpha Particle: $\quad {}_{2}^{4}\alpha$ or ${}_{2}^{4}He$

$$\Delta E = \Delta mc^2 \qquad \Delta m \text{ in kg} \qquad c = 2.9979 \cdot 10^8 \text{ m/s}$$

$$A = A_0 e^{-kt} \qquad k = \frac{0.693}{HL} \qquad \text{(Reference Page 88)}$$

Basics of Physics

Force (Newtons)

$$F = ma \qquad\qquad F_x = ma_x \text{ (X direction)} \qquad\qquad F_y = ma_y \text{ (Y direction)}$$

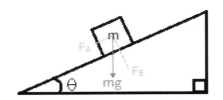

$$F_A = mg \sin\theta$$

$$F_B = mg \cos\theta$$

Position (m), Velocity (m/s), and Acceleration (m/s²)

$$x = x_0 + v_0 t + \frac{1}{2}at^2 \qquad\qquad \Delta x = \frac{1}{2}\left(v_{fx} + v_{ix}\right)\Delta t$$

$$v = v_0 + at \qquad\qquad (v_f)^2 = (v_i)^2 + 2a\Delta x$$

Subscripts denote special properties of the variable like either initial or final, x or y direction, and/or array values.

Circular Motion

θ is similar to x and y $\qquad\qquad$ ω is similar to v $\qquad\qquad$ α is similar to a

$$\theta = \theta_0 + \omega_0 t + \frac{1}{2}\alpha t^2 \qquad\qquad \Delta\theta = \frac{1}{2}\left(\omega_f + \omega_i\right)\Delta t$$

$$\omega = \omega_0 + \alpha t \qquad\qquad (\omega_f)^2 = (\omega_i)^2 + 2\alpha\Delta\theta$$

Arc Length	Linear Velocity	Tangential Acc.	Radial Acc.
$s = r\theta$	$v = r|\omega|$	$a_t = r|\alpha|$	$a_r = \omega^2 r$

Basics of Physics

Energy

Kinetic Energy: $\quad KE = \frac{1}{2}mv^2$ $\qquad$ Potential Energy: $PE = mgh$

Kinetic Energy is energy in motion and Potential Energy is stored energy.

$$W = F\Delta r \cos\theta \qquad\qquad\qquad P = F\vec{v}\cos\theta$$

$$KE_i + PE_i = KE_f + PE_f$$

Momentum

$$\rho = mv \qquad\qquad\qquad \Delta\rho = \sum F\Delta t$$

Rotational Applications

$$W = \tau\Delta\theta \qquad\qquad\qquad \sum\tau = I\alpha \quad \text{(Think: } F = ma)$$

$$KE = \frac{1}{2}Mv^2 + \frac{1}{2}I\omega^2$$

Simple Harmonic Motion

$$x = A\cos\omega t \qquad x = A\sin\omega t \qquad v_{max} = \omega A$$
$$v_x = -v_{max}\sin\omega t \qquad v_x = v_{max}\cos\omega t \qquad a_{max} = \omega^2 A$$
$$a_x = -a_{max}\cos\omega t \qquad a_x = -a_{max}\sin\omega t \qquad ME = \frac{1}{2}kA^2$$

$$\omega = \sqrt{\frac{k}{m}} \qquad\qquad \omega = \sqrt{\frac{g}{L}} \qquad\qquad \omega = \sqrt{\frac{mgd}{I}}$$

Basics of Physics

<u>Two Triangles</u>

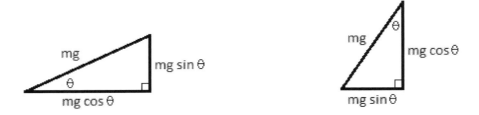

The two triangles above are helpful in several instances involving an angled force of gravity.

Author's Note: I included only a few techniques from Physics due to the lack of special techniques within the subject. I have tutored Physics for about two years and have yet to find as many special techniques compared to the number of techniques found within Math and Chemistry. Mainly, Physics has numerous equations and sub-variations of equations which make it difficult to categorize special techniques.

Word Problems (Level Three)

Level three word problems are exercises that require multiple equation manipulations and insight. Sometimes, the exercises would not contain a direct path to the objective. The first two exercises here would be from General Physics.

Ex. 1: A vehicle is accelerating at a constant rate. A pendulum within the vehicle is producing an angle of 24° in the figure below while in motion. What is the acceleration of the vehicle?

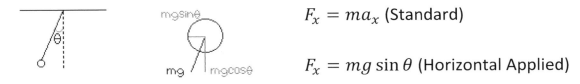

$$F_x = ma_x \text{ (Standard)}$$

$$F_x = mg \sin \theta \text{ (Horizontal Applied)}$$

Author's Note: Notice that the standard equation contains mass and acceleration while the horizontal force applied to the pendulum is $mg \sin \theta$, both of which contain mass. Usually, mass would have been given along with force to obtain acceleration. Since we were not given mass, we obtain two force equations which will allow us to obtain acceleration without mass.

$$ma_x = mg \sin \theta \rightarrow a_x = g \sin \theta \rightarrow a_x = (9.80 \text{ m/s}^2) \sin(24°) \rightarrow \mathbf{3.99 \text{ m/s}^2}$$

Ex. 2: An object with an initial velocity of 7.50 m/s has an initial kinetic energy of 360.0 J. If the object speeds up to 37.5 m/s, what would be the objects final kinetic energy?

$$v_1 = 7.50 \text{ m/s} \qquad KE_1 = 360.0 \text{ J} \qquad v_2 = 37.5 \text{ m/s}$$
$$m \text{ is constant}$$

$$KE = \frac{1}{2}mv^2 \rightarrow \frac{KE_2}{KE_1} = \frac{\frac{1}{2}mv_2^2}{\frac{1}{2}mv_1^2} \rightarrow \frac{KE_2}{KE_1} = \frac{v_2^2}{v_1^2} \rightarrow \frac{KE_2}{(360.0)} = \frac{(37.5)^2}{(7.50)^2} \rightarrow KE_2 = \frac{(360.0)(37.5)^2}{(7.50)^2}$$

$$KE_2 = 9000 \text{ J} \rightarrow KE_2 = \mathbf{9.00 \text{ kJ}}$$

Word Problems (Level Three)

Ex. 3: The instantaneous acceleration for an object is $a(t) = 12t + 6$ and the object's initial velocity is 3 meters per second and the object's initial position is 10 meters. Find the instantaneous acceleration, the instantaneous velocity, and the object's position after 16 seconds.

Reference: $a(t) = \dfrac{dv}{dt}$ $v(t) = \dfrac{dx}{dt}$

$a(t) = 12t + 6 \rightarrow \dfrac{dv}{dt} = 12t + 6 \rightarrow dv = (12t + 6)\,dt \rightarrow$
$\int dv = \int (12t + 6)\,dt \rightarrow v = 6t^2 + 6t + v_0 \rightarrow v(t) = 6t^2 + 6t + 3$

$v(t) = 6t^2 + 6t + 3 \rightarrow \dfrac{dx}{dt} = 6t^2 + 6t + 3 \rightarrow dx = (6t^2 + 6t + 3)\,dt$
$\int dx = \int (6t^2 + 6t + 3)\,dt \rightarrow x = 2t^3 + 3t^2 + 3t + x_0 \rightarrow$
$x(t) = 2t^3 + 3t^2 + 3t + 10$

When $t = 16$ s

$a(16) = 12(16) + 6 \rightarrow$ **198 m/s^2**

$v(16) = 6(16)^2 + 6(16) + 3 \rightarrow$ **1635 m/s**

$x(16) = 2(16)^3 + 3(16)^2 + 3(16) + 10 \rightarrow$ **9018 m**

In example 3 above, the exercise involves techniques within Calculus, specifically Implicit Differentiation and Integration. This is required whenever acceleration is not constant. However, this is utilized within deeper Physics courses.

Let's Bake Some Cookies!

Author's Note: I have tutored students within many subjects and through many situations. Selecting and describing a Math, Chemistry, or Physics session may not be applicable to the average reader. So I have selected to describe a tutoring session through a more common application.

On a day away from tutoring Math and Science, Will selected to enjoy the company of his family. The festivities of the family can vary depending on the mood and occasion. This day in particular, Alice and Olivia wanted to learn how to bake cookies just as good as Will. Delighted about the little ones' curiosity, Will decided to teach them his recipe and baking technique.

First, the following ingredients must be acquired and measured:

2 ¼ cups of flour

1 tsp. of salt

1 tsp. of baking soda

¾ cups of granulated sugar

¾ cups of light brown sugar

1 cup (2 sticks) of butter

1 tsp. of vanilla extract

2 large eggs

2 cups of semi-sweet chocolate chips

Second, the following equipment must be acquired:

2 cookie sheets

2 mixing bowls

2 measuring cups (1 cup and ¼ cup)

1 measuring spoon (1 tsp.)

1 large mixing utensil

1 spoon

Parchment Paper

Let's Bake Some Cookies!

After Will obtained the proper ingredients and equipment, he contemplated how to express the procedure to Alice and Olivia. Will decided to list out and describe the details of the procedure through phases.

Phase 1: Mixing the dry ingredients.

"Take 2 ¼ cups of flour using both the 1 and ¼ measuring cups and add into a bowl (twice with the 1 cup and once with the ¼ cup). Within the same bowl, add 1 tsp of salt and 1 tsp of baking soda using the measuring spoon. Once all three are placed into the bowl, mix well with the large mixing utensil (large spoon or fork will work just fine)."

Will, Alice, and Olivia began to set up the kitchen while the rest of the children played in and out of the house sporadically. As Will began to scoop out the cups of flour, Logan and Wyatt, both taking a break from playing with the other children and wanting to help, enthusiastically grip the bag of flour simultaneously; in which caused a cloud of flour to blast onto Will. Once the cloud settled, Will realized that an exact cup of flour was extracted from the bag. Humored by this even within the chaos caused, Will simply laughed and added the cup of flour to the mixing bowl. As Will dusted himself off, Olivia proceeded to add the teaspoons of salt and baking soda. Once all three were added to the bowl, Olivia began to mix the ingredients.

Phase 2: Mixing the wet ingredients.

"In the second bowl, add 1 cup (2 sticks) of butter brought to about room temperature (this should soften the butter enough for mixing). Next, add ¾ cups of granulated sugar using the ¼ measuring cup (three ¼ cups). Once the granulated sugar has been added, add ¾ cups of light brown sugar using the ¼ measuring cup (again, three ¼ cups). Keep in mind that the light brown sugar should be compacted into the ¼ cup to properly obtain a full ¼ cup. Finally, add 1 tsp of vanilla extract using the measuring spoon. Mix all four thoroughly."

Let's Bake Some Cookies!

Will added the butter into a second bowl once it had reached the proper temperature. Alice then measured out and added the granulated sugar. Next, Alice carefully measured and added the light brown sugar. Then, Will began to add the vanilla extract, making sure not to add too much or too little. Once all four were in the bowl, Alice began to mix the ingredients thoroughly.

Phase 3: Add the eggs.

"Once the first four wet ingredients are mixed, add one large egg and mix (Be careful not to over mix). Once the first egg is mixed into the batter, add one more large egg and mix (Again, be careful not to over mix)."

With the wet ingredients mixed, Will looks to the fridge for two large eggs. Oddly, Will was having difficulty finding the eggs. After a few moments, Madison walks up and showed Will where the two eggs were hidden within the fridge. Neutral of who hid the eggs, Will proceeded to mix the eggs, one by one, into the wet ingredients.

Phase 4: Adding the dry ingredients into the wet ingredients.

"Slowly add small portions of the dry ingredients into the wet ingredients in 5 separate steps. For instance, add one fifth of the dry ingredients into the wet ingredients and mix well. Once mixed, add another one fifth of the dry ingredients into the wet ingredients and mix well. Repeat this process till all the dry ingredients are added into the wet ingredients."

For this phase, Will mixed the ingredients while Alice and Olivia helped add the dry ingredients into the wet ingredients. Even though Alice and Olivia offered to help with the mixing, Will declined and explained that the cookie batter at this point became rather difficult to mix. Still, Will thanked his sweet nieces for helping him with baking cookies and wanted them to continue observing his technique so they can one day master it.

Let's Bake Some Cookies!

Phase 5: Add the semi-sweet chocolate chips!

"Add 2 cups of semi-sweet chocolate chips and mix well."

Will began to add chocolate chips in the following matter: cup for the bowl, cup for Will, cup for the bowl, cup for Will. After the laughter of the children settled, Will placed back some of the chocolate chips designated to him back in its respective container, and began to mix all the ingredients that were in the bowl.

Phase 6: Baking

"Cover the cookie batter and set the oven to 375 degrees Fahrenheit. While the oven is heating up, add Parchment Paper onto the cookie sheets and set away from the oven. Using the spoon, add a dozen dollops of cookie batter each approximately one inch in diameter onto each combination of Parchment Paper and cookie sheet. Essentially, scoop and measure with the spoon and drop the cookie batter onto the Parchment Paper without additional shaping; do this 12 times for each cookie sheet. Once the oven reaches the desired temperature, place **one** of the prepared cookie sheets into the oven and bake for approximately 9-10 minutes. Investigate this thoroughly as baking times can vary.

Once the dozen in the oven is finished baking, set it aside the away from the oven, carefully remove the Parchment Paper with cookies onto a cooling area. Let the hot cookie sheet cool down before adding Parchment Paper and cookie batter. Place the other prepared and cool cookie sheet into the oven.

Repeat the preparation of dozen dollops of cookie batter onto cookie sheets until all the batter is used. Be sure the cookie sheet is cool before repeating the process."

Let's Bake Some Cookies!

Once the batter began to rest, Will started preparations to bake. With the children (and adults) eagerly awaiting for cookies, Will transcended into a meditative trance as he began to carefully place cookie batter onto the Parchment Paper and cookie sheets. Once the oven was heated, Will placed the first dozen cookies into the oven. Keeping track of the time and his senses, Will sensed when the cookies finished baking.

Will took out the first set of cookies and set them aside to cool. As Will placed the next dozen cookies into the oven, Mason elected to take one of the hot cookies and immediately proceeded to eat the cookie. Once finished, Mason exclaimed the slight pain from the hot cookie was worth it. Knowing well how amazing gooey cookies fresh from the oven can be, Will definitely can relate...only Will would have waiting an extra moment or two to allow the cookie to cool. After a couple moments of deep thought, Will reached out for a cookie, only to notice that all the cookies were already taken. This was not surprising to Will as such cookies are easily consumed when the family out-numbered the amount of cookies available.

As Will continued to bake, Alice and Olivia asked how Will was able to detect when the cookies were done. Will explained that since he had baked cookies countless times, he began to notice the perfect pattern to how long cookies required to bake to perfection. Then Will also explained that in fact, with so much practice baking cookies he was able to master the technique to baking cookies.

Once the final cookies were taken out of the oven, Will realized that only a few cookies were left. As Will thought about if he should bake more cookies, the last of the cookies vanished. Will laughed and confirmed his decision to bake more cookies. Will asked if Alice and Olivia wanted to bake more cookies. Delighted to help again, Alice and Olivia began to help Will bake more cookies.

Let's Bake Some Cookies!

Author's Note: Ask anyone that has enjoyed my cookies and they will confirm that my cookies are some of the best cookies they have had. In fact, during the holiday season I tend to bake about 1000+ cookies for family and friends. I much enjoy baking for others! Granted, I am sure there are bakers that have better recipes and better techniques then me, but that's the beauty of learning. I can always improve my recipes and techniques.

As for the techniques within this journal, I have sharpened them to the best of my abilities. In fact, between the second and third draft of this journal, I discovered further improvements for several techniques. I was able to strengthen the techniques within this journal through rigorous practice and experimentation. Such techniques cannot be mastered without practice. The same can be said with any skill or craft, especially with a common day task such as baking cookies.

For those who wish to improve themselves, be ready to practice long and hard. All skills (physical, mental, and spiritual) require great practice to master. Math and Science is especially no exception to this rule. Looking for a quicker and easier solution tends to yield chaos and lost time. Focus on your strengths and improve them beyond your limits. No matter the dream you are chasing, you are required to keep improving yourself to strengthen your chances for your dream.

After all, even a master can use a little more practice.

Learning Styles

Within the Beginner Tutor section of this journal, I mentioned the learning styles within students as follows: Sensory Command, Abstract Aptitude, Imaginative Imagery, and Theory Crafting/Execution.

I have become aware of the limitations students have in regards to learning Math and Science. Students have become more inclined to the ideology of labeling themselves as Visual Learners, Audio Learners, or Kinesthetic Learners. This has given students an excuse to only focus on one set of techniques within the aforementioned labels. As a consequence, the label selected only designates techniques that stimulate that one sense. Such narrow-mindedness has given students far less inclination to invest into the other senses; furthermore, students are then less inclined to invest into other forms of learning.

The main issue a student would have within the disciplines of Math and Science is the student's lack of insight. I believe this is mainly due to the student having narrow-mindedness and lack of vigorous practice. Within the disciplines of Math and Science, simply seeing, hearing, and writing while working out the exercises does little to truly influence one's insight. One must gather a deeper understanding as to why the process of working out an exercise is executed and implemented.

Sensory Command is only the introductory level to learning. Sensory Command describes the five main senses humans have: sight, hearing, touch, smell, and taste. Primarily, the senses of sight, hearing, and touch are used in working out Math and Science exercises. The senses of smell and taste are less implemented in regards to calculations. Although, in the Let's Make Cookies chapter, the Chemistry experiment of baking cookies does delightfully require smell and taste. Not to mention, baking cookies required following a recipe and procedure no doubt required vigorous experimentation and analysis to obtain.

Learning Styles

Abstract Aptitude is another form of learning involving the ability to calculate and analyze any given scenario. Within the subjects of Algebra, Trigonometry, and Calculus require students to solve exercises through the use of techniques and formulas. Obtaining Abstract Aptitude does require vigorous practice and meditation as this would be the inner workings within calculations. The cookie recipe itself was obtained through calculation and experimentation. Also, modifying the recipe would require more calculation to adjust proportions and ingredients. For instance, one modification would be to switch the one teaspoon vanilla extract with three teaspoons of cinnamon and one teaspoon of coriander to change the chocolate-chip cookie into a cinnamon-chocolate-chip cookie.

Imaginative Imagery is the ability to picture any given situation into one's own mind. Articulating Imaginative Imagery is not an easy task as the tutor would only have the ability to project imagery through hand drawn illustrations or through verbally describing the situation. The student himself or herself must construct his or her Imaginative Imagery within themselves. One must practice imagination to the extent in creating the situations portrayed in the exercises. For the recipe modification, I thought of using four teaspoons of cinnamon as opposed to one teaspoon of vanilla extract. I thought of how it would taste and I realized that the cinnamon would overpower the chocolate in that proportion. After the simulated imagery, I decided to alter the modification to three teaspoons of cinnamon and one teaspoon of coriander.

Learning Styles

Theory Crafting/Execution involves the ability to create a procedure and to execute the procedure in problem solving. With the use and practice of the other three categories of learning styles, the student himself or herself should begin to obtain the ability to craft and execute mental procedures for the exercises within Math and Science. The experience of the student also plays a vital role in Theory Crafting/Execution as the student should be exposed to many problem solving situations in order to ingest the metaphorical puzzle pieces to solving unique problems. Once I elected to use the cinnamon-coriander modification, I followed the procedure described in the Let's Make Cookies chapter, except I added the cinnamon and coriander instead of the vanilla extract. To confirm my theory, I enjoyed my newly formed cookies and kept a mental note on any further improvements I can make on my "cookie craft".

One must embrace and be adaptive to these learning styles and others with an open mind. Only after vigorous practice, adaptability, and meditation will one truly obtain insight.

Author's Note: The Learning Styles mentioned are not limited to use within Math and Science. Learning Styles can be used to solve virtually any exercise or problem within any discipline. Also, the Learning Styles mentioned are my personal analysis among the many students I have tutored.

Students may feel rather overwhelmed to this form of thinking as this form of thinking requires time and devotion to master. The two main issues to this is time management and narrow-mindedness students tend to have during their college career. Such aforementioned barriers (among others) must be overcome in order for the student to ascend their insight.

Students and tutors alike must remain patient as the pursuit to enlightenment takes time and great effort.

Appendix A

Pascal's Triangle

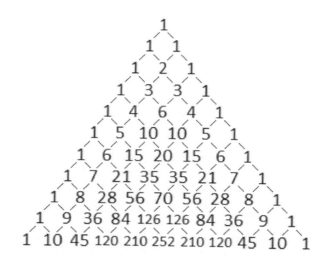

Notice the values within Pascal's Triangle match the values when using $C(n, r)$.

$$C(8,3) = 56 \qquad\qquad C(10,4) = 210$$

This information can be very useful when dealing with Probability, Binomial Theorem, and other applications involving $C(n, r)$.

$$(x + y)^5 = x^5 + 5x^4y + 10x^3y^2 + 10x^2y^3 + 5xy^4 + y^5$$

The coefficients match one of the levels of Pascal's Triangle; more specifically, five levels below the top (1, 5, 10, 10, 5, 1).

Appendix B

Z-Table

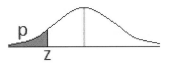

Z	=	p	Z	=	p	Z	=	p
-3.40	=	0.0003	-2.25	=	0.0122	-1.10	=	0.1357
-3.35	=	0.0004	-2.20	=	0.0139	-1.05	=	0.1469
-3.30	=	0.0005	-2.15	=	0.0158	-1.00	=	0.1587
-3.25	=	0.0006	-2.10	=	0.0179	-0.95	=	0.1711
-3.20	=	0.0007	-2.05	=	0.0202	-0.90	=	0.1841
-3.15	=	0.0008	-2.00	=	0.0228	-0.85	=	0.1977
-3.10	=	0.0010	-1.95	=	0.0256	-0.80	=	0.2119
-3.05	=	0.0011	-1.90	=	0.0287	-0.75	=	0.2266
-3.00	=	0.0013	-1.85	=	0.0322	-0.70	=	0.2420
-2.95	=	0.0016	-1.80	=	0.0359	-0.65	=	0.2578
-2.90	=	0.0019	-1.75	=	0.0401	-0.60	=	0.2743
-2.85	=	0.0022	-1.70	=	0.0446	-0.55	=	0.2912
-2.80	=	0.0026	-1.65	=	0.0495	-0.50	=	0.3085
-2.75	=	0.0030	-1.60	=	0.0548	-0.45	=	0.3264
-2.70	=	0.0035	-1.55	=	0.0606	-0.40	=	0.3446
-2.65	=	0.0040	-1.50	=	0.0668	-0.35	=	0.3632
-2.60	=	0.0047	-1.45	=	0.0735	-0.30	=	0.3821
-2.55	=	0.0054	-1.40	=	0.0808	-0.25	=	0.4013
-2.50	=	0.0062	-1.35	=	0.0885	-0.20	=	0.4207
-2.45	=	0.0071	-1.30	=	0.0968	-0.15	=	0.4404
-2.40	=	0.0082	-1.25	=	0.1056	-0.10	=	0.4602
-2.35	=	0.0094	-1.20	=	0.1151	-0.05	=	0.4801
-2.30	=	0.0107	-1.15	=	0.1251	0.00	=	0.5000

Appendix B

Z-Table

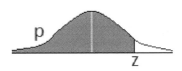

Z	=	p	Z	=	p	Z	=	p
0.00	=	0.5000	1.15	=	0.8749	2.30	=	0.9893
0.05	=	0.5199	1.20	=	0.8849	2.35	=	0.9906
0.10	=	0.5398	1.25	=	0.8944	2.40	=	0.9918
0.15	=	0.5596	1.30	=	0.9032	2.45	=	0.9929
0.20	=	0.5793	1.35	=	0.9115	2.50	=	0.9938
0.25	=	0.5987	1.40	=	0.9192	2.55	=	0.9946
0.30	=	0.6179	1.45	=	0.9265	2.60	=	0.9953
0.35	=	0.6368	1.50	=	0.9332	2.65	=	0.9960
0.40	=	0.6554	1.55	=	0.9394	2.70	=	0.9965
0.45	=	0.6736	1.60	=	0.9452	2.75	=	0.9970
0.50	=	0.6915	1.65	=	0.9505	2.80	=	0.9974
0.55	=	0.7088	1.70	=	0.9554	2.85	=	0.9978
0.60	=	0.7257	1.75	=	0.9599	2.90	=	0.9981
0.65	=	0.7422	1.80	=	0.9641	2.95	=	0.9984
0.70	=	0.7580	1.85	=	0.9678	3.00	=	0.9987
0.75	=	0.7734	1.90	=	0.9713	3.05	=	0.9989
0.80	=	0.7881	1.95	=	0.9744	3.10	=	0.9990
0.85	=	0.8023	2.00	=	0.9772	3.15	=	0.9992
0.90	=	0.8159	2.05	=	0.9798	3.20	=	0.9993
0.95	=	0.8289	2.10	=	0.9821	3.25	=	0.9994
1.00	=	0.8413	2.15	=	0.9842	3.30	=	0.9995
1.05	=	0.8531	2.20	=	0.9861	3.35	=	0.9996
1.10	=	0.8643	2.25	=	0.9878	3.40	=	0.9997

Appendix C

Atomic Mass Unit List

#	Element (Symbol)	Mass	#	Element (Symbol)	Mass
1	Hydrogen (H)	1.008	25	Manganese (Mn)	54.94
2	Helium (He)	4.003	26	Iron (Fe)	55.85
3	Lithium (Li)	6.941	27	Cobalt (Co)	58.93
4	Beryllium (Be)	9.012	28	Nickel (Ni)	58.69
5	Boron (B)	10.81	29	Copper (Cu)	63.55
6	Carbon (C)	12.01	30	Zinc (Zn)	65.39
7	Nitrogen (N)	14.01	31	Gallium (Ga)	69.72
8	Oxygen (O)	16.00	32	Germanium (Ge)	72.64
9	Fluorine (F)	19.00	33	Arsenic (As)	74.92
10	Neon (Ne)	20.18	34	Selenium (Se)	78.97
11	Sodium (Na)	22.99	35	Bromine (Br)	79.90
12	Magnesium (Mg)	24.31	36	Krypton (Kr)	83.80
13	Aluminum (Al)	26.98	37	Rubidium (Rb)	85.47
14	Silicon (Si)	28.09	38	Strontium (Sr)	87.62
15	Phosphorus (P)	30.97	39	Yttrium (Y)	88.91
16	Sulfur (S)	32.07	40	Zirconium (Zr)	91.22
17	Chlorine (Cl)	35.45	41	Niobium (Nb)	92.91
18	Argon (Ar)	39.95	42	Molybdenum (Mo)	95.95
19	Potassium (K)	39.10	43	Technetium (Tc)	(98)
20	Calcium (Ca)	40.08	44	Ruthenium (Ru)	101.1
21	Scandium (Sc)	44.96	45	Rhodium (Rh)	102.9
22	Titanium (Ti)	47.87	46	Palladium (Pd)	106.4
23	Vanadium (V)	50.94	47	Silver (Ag)	107.9
24	Chromium (Cr)	52.00	48	Cadmium (Cd)	112.4

Appendix C

Atomic Mass Unit List

#	Element (Symbol)	Mass	#	Element (Symbol)	Mass
49	Indium (In)	114.8	73	Tantalum (Ta)	180.9
50	Tin (Sn)	118.7	74	Tungsten (W)	183.8
51	Antimony (Sb)	121.8	75	Rhenium (Re)	186.2
52	Tellurium (Te)	127.6	76	Osmium (Os)	190.2
53	Iodine (I)	126.9	77	Iridium (Ir)	192.2
54	Xenon (Xe)	131.3	78	Platinum (Pt)	195.1
55	Cesium (Cs)	132.9	79	Gold (Au)	197.0
56	Barium (Ba)	137.3	80	Mercury (Hg)	200.6
57	Lanthanum (La)	138.9	81	Thallium (Tl)	204.4
58	Cerium (Ce)	140.1	82	Lead (Pb)	207.2
59	Praseodymium (Pr)	140.9	83	Bismuth (Bi)	209.0
60	Neodymium (Nd)	144.2	84	Polonium (Po)	(209)
61	Promethium (Pm)	(145)	85	Astatine (At)	(210)
62	Samarium (Sm)	150.4	86	Radon (Rn)	(222)
63	Europium (Eu)	152.0	87	Francium (Fr)	(223)
64	Gadolinium (Gd)	157.3	88	Radium (Ra)	(226)
65	Terbium (Tb)	158.9	89	Actinium (Ac)	(227)
66	Dysprosium (Dy)	162.5	90	Thorium (Th)	232.0
67	Holmium (Ho)	164.9	91	Protactinium (Pa)	231.0
68	Erbium (Er)	167.3	92	Uranium (U)	238.0
69	Thulium (Tm)	168.9	93	Neptunium (Np)	(237)
70	Ytterbium (Yb)	173.0	94	Plutonium (Pu)	(244)
71	Lutetium (Lu)	175.0			
72	Hafnium (Hf)	178.5	95-118 (Synthetic Elements)		

Appendix D

Trigonometric Identities

$$\tan \theta = \frac{\sin \theta}{\cos \theta} \qquad \cot \theta = \frac{\cos \theta}{\sin \theta}$$

$$\csc \theta = \frac{1}{\sin \theta} \qquad \sec \theta = \frac{1}{\cos \theta} \qquad \cot \theta = \frac{1}{\tan \theta}$$

$$\sin^2 \theta + \cos^2 \theta = 1 \qquad \tan^2 \theta + 1 = \sec^2 \theta \qquad \cot^2 \theta + 1 = \csc^2 \theta$$

$$\sin(2\theta) = 2 \sin \theta \cos \theta \qquad \sin\left(\frac{\theta}{2}\right) = \pm\sqrt{\frac{1-\cos\theta}{2}}$$

$$\cos(2\theta) = \cos^2 \theta - \sin^2 \theta \qquad \cos\left(\frac{\theta}{2}\right) = \pm\sqrt{\frac{1+\cos\theta}{2}}$$

$$\cos(2\theta) = 2 \cos^2 \theta - 1 \qquad \tan\left(\frac{\theta}{2}\right) = \pm\sqrt{\frac{1-\cos\theta}{1+\cos\theta}}$$

$$\cos(2\theta) = 1 - 2 \sin^2 \theta \qquad \tan\left(\frac{\theta}{2}\right) = \frac{\sin\theta}{1+\cos\theta}$$

$$\tan(2\theta) = \frac{2 \tan \theta}{1-\tan^2 \theta} \qquad \tan\left(\frac{\theta}{2}\right) = \frac{1-\cos\theta}{\sin\theta}$$

$$\sin(u \pm v) = \sin u \cos v \pm \cos u \sin v$$
$$\cos(u \pm v) = \cos u \cos v \mp \sin u \sin v$$
$$\tan(a \pm v) = \frac{\tan u \pm \tan v}{1 \mp \tan u \tan v}$$

$$\sin u \sin v = \frac{1}{2}[\cos(u - v) - \cos(u + v)]$$
$$\cos u \cos v = \frac{1}{2}[\cos(u - v) + \cos(u + v)]$$
$$\sin u \cos v = \frac{1}{2}[\sin(u + v) + \sin(u - v)]$$
$$\cos u \sin v = \frac{1}{2}[\sin(u + v) - \sin(u - v)]$$

$$\sin u + \sin v = 2 \sin\left(\frac{u+v}{2}\right) \cos\left(\frac{u-v}{2}\right)$$
$$\sin u - \sin v = 2 \sin\left(\frac{u-v}{2}\right) \cos\left(\frac{u+v}{2}\right)$$
$$\cos u + \cos v = 2 \cos\left(\frac{u+v}{2}\right) \cos\left(\frac{u-v}{2}\right)$$
$$\cos u - \cos v = -2 \sin\left(\frac{u+v}{2}\right) \sin\left(\frac{u-v}{2}\right)$$

Appendix E

Calculus Identities

$$\frac{d}{dx}[uv] = u'v + uv'$$

$$\frac{d}{dx}\left[\frac{u}{v}\right] = \frac{u'v - uv'}{v^2}$$

$$\frac{d}{dx}[f(u)] = f'(u) \cdot u'$$

$$\frac{d}{dx}[e^u] = u'e^u$$

$$\frac{d}{dx}[\ln u] = \frac{u'}{u}$$

$$\frac{d}{dx}[\sin u] = \cos u \cdot u'$$

$$\frac{d}{dx}[\cos u] = -\sin u \cdot u'$$

$$\frac{d}{dx}[\tan u] = \sec^2 u \cdot u'$$

$$\frac{d}{dx}[\cot u] = -\csc^2 u \cdot u'$$

$$\frac{d}{dx}[\sec u] = \sec u \tan u \cdot u'$$

$$\frac{d}{dx}[\csc u] = -\csc u \cot u \cdot u'$$

$$\frac{d}{dx}[\sin^{-1} u] = \frac{u'}{\sqrt{1-u^2}}$$

$$\frac{d}{dx}[\cos^{-1} u] = -\frac{u'}{\sqrt{1-u^2}}$$

$$\frac{d}{dx}[\tan^{-1} u] = \frac{u'}{1+u^2}$$

$$\frac{d}{dx}[\cot^{-1} u] = -\frac{u'}{1+u^2}$$

$$\frac{d}{dx}[\sec^{-1} u] = \frac{u'}{|u|\sqrt{u^2-1}}$$

$$\frac{d}{dx}[\csc^{-1} u] = -\frac{u'}{|u|\sqrt{u^2-1}}$$

$$\frac{d}{dx}[a^u] = a^u \ln a \cdot u'$$

$$\frac{d}{dx}[\log_a u] = \frac{u'}{u \ln a}$$

$$\int du = u + c$$

$$\int u^n \, du = \frac{1}{n+1} u^{n+1} + c$$

$$\int k \, du = ku + c$$

$$\int \frac{1}{u} du = \ln|u| + c$$

$$\int \cos u \, du = \sin u + c$$

$$\int \sin u \, du = -\cos u + c$$

$$\int \sec^2 u \, du = \tan u + c$$

$$\int \csc^2 u \, du = -\cot u + c$$

$$\int \sec u \tan u \, du = \sec u + c$$

$$\int \csc u \cot u \, du = -\csc u + c$$

$$\int \tan u \, du = -\ln|\cos u| + c$$

$$\int \cot u \, du = \ln|\sin u| + c$$

$$\int \sec u \, du = \ln|\sec u + \tan u| + c$$

$$\int \csc u \, du = \ln|\csc u - \cot u| + c$$

$$\int e^u \, du = e^u + c$$

$$\int a^u \, du = \frac{a^u}{\ln a} + c$$

$$\int \frac{du}{\sqrt{a^2-u^2}} = \sin^{-1}\left(\frac{u}{a}\right) + c$$

$$\int \frac{du}{a^2+u^2} = \frac{1}{a}\tan^{-1}\left(\frac{u}{a}\right) + c$$

$$\int \frac{du}{u\sqrt{u^2-a^2}} = \frac{1}{a}\sec^{-1}\left(\frac{u}{a}\right) + c$$

Appendix F

Chemistry Equations

$$C = \frac{5}{9}(F - 32) \qquad F = \frac{9}{5}C + 32 \qquad K = C + 273.15$$

$$M_1V_1 = M_2V_2 \qquad M_1V_1 + M_2V_2 = M_3V_3$$

$$KE = \frac{1}{2}mv^2 \qquad q = mC\Delta T \qquad q = C\Delta T \text{ (Calorimeter)}$$

$$c = \lambda v \qquad E = hv \qquad E = (-2.178 \cdot 10^{-18})\left(\frac{1}{(n_f)^2} - \frac{1}{(n_i)^2}\right)$$

$$\frac{P_1V_1}{n_1T_1} = \frac{P_2V_2}{n_2T_2} \qquad PV = nRT \qquad d = \frac{PM}{RT}$$

$$X_i = \frac{n_i}{n_{total}} = \frac{P_i}{P_{total}} \qquad u_{rms} = \sqrt{\frac{3RT}{M}} \qquad \frac{r_1}{r_2} = \sqrt{\frac{M_2}{M_1}}$$

$$\ln\left(\frac{P_1}{P_2}\right) = \frac{\Delta H_{vap}}{R}\left(\frac{1}{T_2} - \frac{1}{T_1}\right), R = 8.314 \frac{\text{J}}{\text{mol K}}$$

$$FP_f = FP_i - \Delta T_f \qquad BP_f = BP_i + \Delta T_b$$

$$\Delta T_f = ik_f m \qquad \Delta T_b = ik_b m \qquad \pi = iMRT$$

$$rate = -\frac{1}{a} \cdot \frac{\Delta[A]}{\Delta t} = -\frac{1}{b} \cdot \frac{\Delta[B]}{\Delta t} = \frac{1}{c} \cdot \frac{\Delta[C]}{\Delta t} = \frac{1}{d} \cdot \frac{\Delta[D]}{\Delta t} \qquad rate = k[A]^m[B]^n$$

$$\text{First Order:} \qquad \ln[A_t] = -kt + \ln[A_0] \qquad t_{\frac{1}{2}} = \frac{\ln 2}{k}$$

$$\text{Second Order:} \qquad \frac{1}{[A_t]} = kt + \frac{1}{[A_0]} \qquad t_{\frac{1}{2}} = \frac{1}{k[A_0]}$$

$$k = Ae^{\left(-\frac{E_a}{RT}\right)} \qquad \ln\left(\frac{k_1}{k_2}\right) = \left(-\frac{E_a}{R}\right)\left(\frac{1}{T_1} - \frac{1}{T_2}\right)$$

$$\text{pH} = -\log[H_3O^+] \qquad [H_3O^+] = 10^{-\text{pH}} \qquad \text{pH} + \text{pOH} = 14$$

$$\text{pOH} = -\log[OH^-] \qquad [OH^-] = 10^{-\text{pOH}} \qquad \text{pH} = pK_a + \log\left(\frac{[A^-]}{[HA]}\right)$$

$$S = k\ln W, W = n^x \qquad \Delta S_{surroundings} = -\frac{\Delta H_{system}}{T}$$

$$\Delta G = \Delta H - T\Delta S \qquad \Delta G = \Delta G° + RT\ln Q \qquad \Delta G° = -RT\ln K$$

$$\Delta G = -nFE_{cell} \qquad E°_{cell} = \frac{RT}{nF}\ln K \qquad E = E°_{cell} - \frac{RT}{nF}\ln Q$$

Appendix G

Physics Equations

$$F = ma \qquad F_x = ma_x \text{ (X direction)} \qquad F_y = ma_y \text{ (Y direction)}$$

$$x = x_0 + v_0 t + \frac{1}{2}at^2 \qquad\qquad \Delta x = \frac{1}{2}(v_{fx} + v_{ix})\Delta t$$
$$v = v_0 + at \qquad\qquad (v_f)^2 = (v_i)^2 + 2a\Delta x$$

$$\theta = \theta_0 + \omega_0 t + \frac{1}{2}\alpha t^2 \qquad\qquad \Delta\theta = \frac{1}{2}(\omega_f + \omega_i)\Delta t$$
$$\omega = \omega_0 + \alpha t \qquad\qquad (\omega_f)^2 = (\omega_i)^2 + 2\alpha\Delta\theta$$
$$s = r\theta \qquad v = r|\omega| \qquad a_t = r|\alpha| \qquad a_r = \omega^2 r$$

$$KE = \frac{1}{2}mv^2 \qquad PE = mgh \qquad KE_i + PE_i = KE_f + PE_f$$
$$W = F\Delta r \cos\theta \qquad P = F\vec{v}\cos\theta$$

$$\rho = mv \qquad\qquad \Delta\rho = \sum F\Delta t$$

$$W = \tau\Delta\theta \qquad \sum\tau = I\alpha \qquad KE = \frac{1}{2}Mv^2 + \frac{1}{2}I\omega^2$$

$$x = A\cos\omega t \qquad x = A\sin\omega t \qquad v_{max} = \omega A$$
$$v_x = -v_{max}\sin\omega t \qquad v_x = v_{max}\cos\omega t \qquad a_{max} = \omega^2 A$$
$$a_x = -a_{max}\cos\omega t \qquad a_x = -a_{max}\sin\omega t \qquad ME = \frac{1}{2}kA^2$$

$$\omega = \sqrt{\frac{k}{m}} \qquad\qquad \omega = \sqrt{\frac{g}{L}} \qquad\qquad \omega = \sqrt{\frac{mgd}{I}}$$

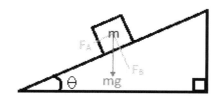

$$F_A = mg\sin\theta$$

$$F_B = mg\cos\theta$$

Made in the USA
San Bernardino, CA
18 March 2019